MW00512757

DAY TRADING GUIDE FOR BEGINNERS 2020

LEARN THE BASICS, THE BEST STRATEGIES AND ADVANCED TECHNIQUES ON HOW TO TRADE FOR A LIVING PENNY STOCKS, OPTIONS, FOREX WITH THE RIGHT MARKET INVESTING PSYCHOLOGY.

Table of Contents

Introduction

Before we get into the meat of day trading and making money off it, we'll have to cover the basics first. In particular, we'll need to learn what day trading is and the things you'll need for it. In this chapter, we'll focus on what day trading is.

What Is Day Trading?

Day trading is a strategy of trading financial securities, such as stocks and currencies, where positions are taken and closed within the same day. Also called short trading, it involves buying a financial security and selling them before the trading day closes.

How short can day trading last? It can be as short as buying and selling in a few minutes, or even seconds! The point is to end the trading day with a square position, i.e., neither long nor short on any financial security.

It doesn't matter how many trades you do during the day. You can trade just once a day or 10 times a day...it doesn't matter. The defining characteristic of day trading is ending the day with a square position.

Day trading can take place in any market, but the most common ones are the stock market and foreign exchange or forex markets.

When you start day trading, you'll need to start looking at financial securities from a different vantage point. For example, if you're used to swing trading or a buy-and-hold approach to stock market investing, you'll need to look at stocks differently when you day trade if you want to profit from it.

Instead of having a longer-term perspective on stocks, you'll need to reorient it to a very short-term one. In particular, you should shift your focus from a company's possible growth over the long term to its possible immediate price actions during the day.

Another area where you'll need to reorient your thinking are gains. Instead of looking at substantial gains, e.g., 10% or more, you'll need to scale down. Given the short time frame, you may have to make do with gains as low as 1% to 2%. This is because day trading involves trading at a higher frequency but with smaller gains, which accumulate over time.

How to Day Trade

Once you start day trading, you can use a myriad number of techniques and methods to execute trades. For example, you can choose to trade based solely on your "gut feeling" or you can go to the other extreme of relying entirely on mathematical models that optimize trading success through elaborate automated trading systems.

Regardless of the method, you can have limitless day-trading profit potential once you master day trading. Here are some of the strategies many expert day traders use profitably.

One is what's called "trading the news", which is one of the most popular day trading strategies since time immemorial. As you may have already gleaned from the name, it involves acting upon any press-released information such as economic data, interest rates, and corporate earnings.

Another popular day trading strategy is called "fading the gap at the open". This one's applicable on trading days when a security's price opens with a gap, i.e., below the previous day's lowest price or above the previous day's highest price.

"Fading the gap at the open" means taking an opposite position from the gap's direction. If the price opens with a downward gap, i.e., below the previous day's lowest price, you buy the security. If the price opens with an upward gap, i.e., it opens higher than the previous day's highest price, you short or sell the security.

Markets Where You Can Day Trade

For most people, especially the uninitiated, day trading equals stock market trading. They're not entirely wrong because most day traders trade in stocks listed in major stock exchanges. They're not entirely right, too, because there are other markets where day traders also make money. But that being said, let's look at the stock market first, considering it's the most popular market for day trading.

If you'd like to start day trading in the United States' stock market, you'll need a minimum of $25,000 in your broker's account at all times. This means if your equity balance falls below this amount at any point, your day trading privileges may be suspended until you put in more money to meet the minimum amount.

Your equity balance includes your cash balance and the current market value of the stocks you're holding. If the market values of the stocks you're holding plunge to the point that your total equity balance falls below the minimum, you'll be compelled by your broker to put in more money to bring your equity back up to minimum levels.

Considering the highly volatile nature of day trades, you'll be better off starting with an equity balance higher than the minimum. A good amount to start with would be $30,000, which is $5,000 more than the $25,000 minimum most brokers require. With a $5,000 leeway, you won't have to worry about having to frequently put in more money in case the values of your stocks fall.

Another popular day trading market is the futures market. As the name implies, this is the market to trade futures contracts, which are nothing more than formal agreements to buy or sell a specific number or amount of specific assets at a fixed price, regardless of what the price of such assets are in the future.

Day traders can make money day trading futures the same way they do with stocks, i.e., they buy futures contracts at a lower price and sell them at a higher price within the same trading day.

Compared to day trading shares of stocks, day trading futures contracts require less capital. If you want to start day trading the futures market, you'll only need between

$3,500 to $5,000 to begin day trading S&P 500 Emini (ES) contracts, which is one of the best futures to day trade.

Trading hours for futures markets aren't as fixed as those in the stock market. They depend on the kind of contracts involved. For this reason, you must pay close attention to the actual end of trading day for the kind of contracts you're trading to avoid carrying an open position to the next one.

Other day trading markets include the foreign exchange, commodity, and cryptocurrency markets.

How to Choose Your Day Trading Market

There are several things to consider when choosing your day trading market. One of the most important factors is your own financial position. For example, if you can't afford to start trading $30,000, you'll have to skip the stock market and settle for the futures, cryptocurrency, or foreign exchange markets instead.

Another factor to consider is the trading system required to day trade. If you don't have the necessary equipment or software to day trade, you'll be very hard-pressed to succeed in day trading.

Another factor to consider is time zone. You see, the United States isn't the only day trading market that can provide profit opportunities. There are other day trading markets around the world, i.e., different time zones. If you're a night owl, maybe financial markets from the other side of the pond may be more suited for you. If you're a day person, you shouldn't have a problem day trading the United States markets.

And lastly, your personality and interests may also play important roles in your ability to day trade successfully in certain markets. You'll have an easier time learning the ropes of successful day trading markets that you're very interested in compared to markets you don't like.

And when you have finally chosen your starting market, make a commitment to stick to it for the foreseeable future. Why? Flipping back and forth between different markets isn't just stressful, but it can also impede your ability to master a particular market. Focus is key.

Chapter 1 How Day Trading works

What is Day Trading?

* * *

First, let us begin by defining day trading.

As its name suggests, day trading is trading of securities in a day—and I mean every single day as long as the market is open (you will find out about their schedules in a while).

Let us digress for a minute there and break the definition down:

Trading means buying and selling. This is contrary to what many people believe that traders simply sell securities in the market. If the price of the item you wish to buy is low, then it is time to buy. If the value of what you have is high in the market, then you sell. The point here is regardless whether you are buying or selling, your goal is to earn a profit, not a loss.

Securities. Security is defined as any financial asset that you can sell or buy in the market. These include bonds, stocks, and foreign exchange (forex). This can also refer to commodities such as gold, corn, coffee, and gas. Of the many different types of assets that can be traded, two of the most popular for day traders are stocks and foreign exchange.

Stocks are financial instrument or security that signifies your ownership, claim, or stake in a public company. For example, if you buy stocks from McDonald's, it means that you are a part owner of it! As to your privilege, it depends on the stock you have chosen. If it is a preferred stock, then you are guaranteed dividends. An investment in a common stock entitles you to voting rights. The more stocks you have, the bigger your share in the company, although given that there are limitations on how much stocks are available in the public market, the chances of you having huge influence over company decisions is small.

Foreign exchange or forex is trading of different currencies in the market. Three of the most popular currencies traded are US dollar, British sterling pounds, and euro. Various factors can affect the movement of currencies including but not limited to economic growth, natural disasters, terrorism, employment, and even politics.

Day. We also mean this literally since the markets are open as specific times within the day. They are also operating on weekdays and non-holidays.

Retail vs Institutional traders

There are two types of players in day trading: institutional and retail.

Institutional

Institutional traders are those that trade on behalf of companies, such as corporations. They may also participate in the market for the sake of a group like pensioners or people who invest via banks.

One of the biggest distinctions between institutional and retail traders is the complexity of the transactions. Institutional traders handle large potential investments (think of thousands or even millions in a day!). As an example, let us talk about a day trader for mutual funds.

Mutual funds are assets that come from different investors, say, you and your two friends. Each of you contributes a certain amount of money to the fund. Once the ideal amount has been raised, the funds are then traded by a manager or administrator. It is his job to ensure that you earn a profit from your investment as much as possible. Or if the market is not doing well, at least your loss is not a lot. For his work, he gets a small management fee.

Institutional trading can be considered high risk due to the potential huge loss from one wrong decision. However, since the account is also large, these types of traders often have the bargaining power. This means they can negotiate prices and execution directly or through an intermediary, who is called a broker.

They also have:

More access to financial resources and tools

Less worry when it comes to capital or investment funds

Several members that make up the support, research, and analysis team

Retail

Retail traders, meanwhile, are those that invest by piecemeal. But that is not really piecemeal per se since securities like stocks can be sold by lots. To be more specific, if you invest in the stock market and you wish to buy shares, the minimum may be 100, 100, or 1,000 shares, in which each bunch of shares is called a lot. You cannot buy 90, 99, or 999.

Because the securities can be purchased by "piecemeal," the trader can now participate in the market despite his limited funds. In fact, they can trade in small cap stocks or those stocks that have low price prices. This way, the trader has the option to place his capital on many different types of stocks or companies in the market.

A retail trader relies on the assistance and expertise of a broker or an administrator, as in the case of the example above about mutual funds.

Retail traders are not exempted from the loss, and if they play their cards wrong, they can lose everything they have ever invested. However, the loss still remains small compared to that of an institutional trader.

Some financial pundits delegate another group of traders, whom they call as auto traders. These people trade using special computer software and other tools, which usually execute the trader's options and prices. They can also perform complicated analyses, although the actual interpretation still depends on the trader, which is why you need to read this book.

Both retail and institutional traders, however, can also manage the market online.

The Day Trading Time Zones

One of the essential things to keep in mind when you are into day trading is the market schedule. This is the time when the floor is open for buying and selling securities. Now why should this matter to you? Shouldn't you be able to trade at any time during the day? That is actually true!

However, as a trader, your main goal is to MAXIMIZE PROFIT AND MINIMIZE THE LOSS. That can only happen at certain times during the day, not all the time.

As you can see, forex market seems to be open 24 hours a day. But you also have to understand that the market itself does not do anything. Rather, it is the people running and trading in it. For instance, in the American market, the most ideal time to trade is around 9am since this is a period of a very high liquidity. One, by this time, the market is less than volatile unlike the first 20 to 30 minutes of opening time. This is what traders often call the period when the dust has already settled. You can more or less see which ones are gaining and losing. Second, the European market is still open, so there are more traders or players. By late afternoon in New York, the European session has already ended. Further, most of the currencies are traded against the US dollar.

Meanwhile, stocks have a different schedule. New York Stock Exchange (NYSE) trades from Monday to Friday from 9:30am to 4pm ET. It also observes US holidays including Good Friday.

As a trader, however, let me issue this disclaimer: while there are ideal times, there is no guarantee that you will win if you choose to trade at these schedules every time. Again, the market is complex, and many factors can affect the movement of security prices.

Trade the best, leave the rest

In the end, your goal is to make sure that you can say, "It was a successful day." How do you qualify this one? Based on experience, a good successful day trade would be:

Maximum profit

Minimum loss

High liquidity (which means you have sufficient assets for your cash flow)

Diversified portfolio to increase leverage and soften negative impact

Good analysis of fundamental and technical data

Enough data to analyze the market to get yourself prepared once it opens

Day trading is not easy and simple, but it is understandable and, of course, manageable, especially now that you know the basics of it.

Chapter 2 Day Trading Pros and Cons

At its most basic, day trading is just like any other type of securities trading except sped up by a significant degree. Day traders typically only hold specific positions for a few minutes, or less, on average, with no position being held longer than overnight at most. In order to be a successful day trader, you typically need previous experience trading securities in a less high-impact way, dedication to what it is you are trying to do and a high degree of discipline.

The process of making a day trade can be broken down into 5 steps that are going to always be the same regardless of the specifics involved. First you will want to find an asset that you want to trade be it a stock, option, currency pair or any other commonly traded security. You will then decide if it fits your trading plan. If it does you will want to take a specific position based on current market trends. Then you will sell as soon as the desired movement occurs. Finally, you will repeat until you are a veteran day trader.

Pros and cons of day trading

While the above makes day trading sound relatively straightforward, the truth of the matter is that it has a variety of pros and cons that means it is not for everyone. Take a look at the following list to determine if there isn't another type of trading that is better suited to your goals.

The benefits of Day trading

Large profit margins: For those who do it right, day trading can be a very profitable career path with profits that are greater and more reliable than just about any other type of securities trading.

Work for yourself: Many of the most successful day traders are self-employed which means they don't have to answer to anyone, they can make their own hours and set their own profit goals.

Always exciting: Dealing with the shortest market timeframes means that day traders typically see more action than any other type of security trader. You will have the opportunity to pit your wits against the market as well as your competition each and every day. Those who are natural thrill seekers will also appreciate the adrenaline rush that comes from rapid-fire trading and pulling a big win from the grip of defeat.

No degree required: As opposed to many other financial jobs, a perfectly successful day trader can be completely self-taught. As long as you are willing to put in the time and energy to learn the skills you need, you can be a success with no degree required. Everything you need to learn can be found, at very little expense, online.

Tax write off: As self-employed individuals, day traders can write off a great deal of their expenses when it comes time to pay taxes. Sophisticated hardware, expensive software, even home office space can all be partly written off by those who work from home.

The negative of Day trading

Commissions can noticeably affect profits: Due to the higher than average number of trades they make in a single day, the commission cost of individual trades can significantly affect your overall profits if you don't do everything in your power to minimize these costs.

The potential for loss is substantial: Day trading is without a doubt the most difficult of all of the types of securities trading to make a reliable profit in. Most day traders see nothing but losses for a least the first month of their nascent career and if they are not careful these loses can prevent them from ever reaching profit making status. While only trading what you can afford to lose is something that every trader should keep in mind, many new day traders trade with borrowed money in the form of margined trades or capital from loans which can cause them to start out from a significantly indebted position.

High startup costs: Day traders are actively competing against hedge funds, high-frequency traders and other professionals who often have trading capital reserves in the millions. As such, in order to compete it is recommended that you have a trading bankroll that is at least $10,000 at the bare minimum. Additionally, you are going to need to invest upfront in charting software, a trading platform, computer hardware and more. Added to this are the ongoing costs of commissions, live price quotes and other brokerage fees, all of which add up faster than they otherwise would do to the high volume of trades to be made. Finally, many brokerages will not allow you to day trade unless you have proven yourself to be a successful trader on a smaller scale which means there is a time as well as a monetary commitment.

Self-employed: While there are benefits to working for yourself, there are also drawbacks. These include a lack of health insurance, a steady paycheck and corporate infrastructure, just to name a few. This also means that you will need to deal with the isolation that comes from working by yourself with no one around to lend a hand or to make sure you spend your days working instead of browsing social media, you will be completely responsible for your own success. Finally, in order to truly day trade successfully, you need to commit fully from the start which means giving up your steady paycheck to try something far less guaranteed.

Chapter 3 Strategies and say how to use it in the stocks market, forex and options

Options Trading Lingo

Long: If a trader takes a long position that means they purchased a specific stock, option, currency pair etc.

Short: If a trader takes a long position that means they sold a specific stock, option, currency pair etc.

Bear market: If the market is trending downward this is considered a bear market.

Bull market: If the market is trending upward then this is considered a bull market.

Bid price: The bid price is the price that traders are currently buying a given asset for.

Ask price: The ask price is the price that traders are currently selling a given asset for.

Spread: The difference between the ask price and the bid price.

Open: The open price is the price of a given asset at the start of the trading day.

Close: The close price is the price of a given asset at the end of a trading day.

Slippage: The difference between the price of a bid or ask when you decide to make a trade and the actual price when you commit to it.

Intraday range: The difference between the high and low of a given asset between different days.

Volume: The number of shares that trade hands in a given day.

Liquidity: This refers to the ease with which a given security can be obtained. In general, the greater the liquidity, the lower the price.

Volatility: The degree to which the price of a security is likely to change over a specific period of time.

How to find securities to trade

Pre-market movers: While pre-market prices are subject to change once the market opens, they are a great place to start. The first thing you are going to want to look for is a high degree of volume, not just for the day, but for the last 30 days.

Check social media: Social media is often a great place to get a sense of impending news events before they happen. This, in turn will allow you to determine how the market is going to move before it has a chance to get going and let you get in on the ground floor of potential incoming changes.

Earnings calendar: A surefire way to see an increase in volatility is when earnings are reported. You are never going to want to jump on an assumed trend before they are released but shortly thereafter the trade gates will be thrown wide open.

Smart Money vs. Dumb Money

There are two general types of investors. The first is institutional investors. These are large investors like pension funds and hedge funds. Institutional investors are colloquially known as "smart money". They are called smart money because they have more information available and have tools at their disposal like Bloomberg terminals which cost a lot of money while giving them rapid information. Also controlling huge amounts of capital, they can even move the markets.

Retail investors are individual and small traders. This is the "dumb money" – in other words, that is you. Don't take offense, the term doesn't really mean that you are dumb in the sense of being stupid! Dumb money just means that relatively speaking, compared to the large institutional investors you don't have access to the same information at the same speed, so you're not going to be making trades that are as well-informed.

Selling short

Let's begin by looking at a strategy known as selling short. This strategy relies on being able to borrow shares from a broker so that you can profit on the share price decline. The process involves the following steps. First, you'll borrow shares from the broker. Then you sell them on the market. When the share price drops, then you'll buy the shares again, and then you return the shares to the broker.

Of course, this depends on things going in your favor. If the share price doesn't drop, you risk losing money.

To see how you could profit from this, we'll use a simple example. Let's say that ABC is trading at $20 a share at market opening. They're going to release a quarterly report and you're expecting bad news that will make the share price drop, at least for a while. You borrow 100 shares from the broker, and then you immediately sell them. So, you make:

$20 x 100 = $2,000

At this point, it's borrowed money since you must return the shares to the broker. If you're wrong and the price goes up, then you're going to have a loss. But let's say the news comes out and as you expected its very bad news. Say the share price drops to $14. Now you can buy 100 shares at this lower price:

$14 x 100 = $1,400

Then you immediately return the shares to the broker. So, you've made a profit given by:

Price you sold the borrowed shares – Price you paid to get them back = $2,000 - $1,400 = $600 profit.

Not bad eh? Who wouldn't want to make a quick $600 profit in an afternoon just sitting at their computer trading stocks?

Of course, it's not that easy. A lot of speculation goes into day trading, and you can bet wrong, as well as bet right. So maybe you bet wrong and lose $200 instead. Selling short requires that you closely study the stock market and the company you're going to short in order to avoid losses. Selling short may not be the best option for beginning day traders, since the risk that you'll end up owing money is high, even though the potential profits are large.

One or more trades

We've illustrated the process of selling short with a single trade. However, there are more options available. You can trade a given stock multiple times in a single day in the hopes of making profits.

Basic Strategies

Day traders rely on four basic strategies to make daily profits in the stock market. Let's review each of them.

Scalping

Chances are you're familiar with the concept of scalping tickets to an upcoming event, maybe a music concert or high demand sporting event. The idea is you buy the tickets at face value, then when it's sold out you show up at the venue and offer your tickets for sale at a premium price to make a profit.

Scaling isn't the same on the stock market, but scalping is the most basic strategy used by day traders. At its core is the notion of "buy low, sell high". When a day trader uses scalping, they buy the shares at a given price, and then sell immediately when they stand to make a profit. So, if you buy 100 shares of ABC company for $10 a share, a total investment of $10 x 100 = $1,000, you then closely monitor the share price to sell when it becomes profitable. Suppose that at first, it drops to $9.50 a share, and bounces around a bit. Then it jumps up to $11.75 a share. At this point you'll sell right away, earning:

100 shares x $11.75/share = $1,175

Since you invested $1,000 to buy the shares, you've made a quick profit of $175. Scalping is a good way to get your feet wet with day trading, it's a very basic strategy. Of course, you're not going to get into scalping on a random basis, you're going to want to study the markets, keeping up with financial news, and choosing companies that are likely to show an increase in share price that day. This illustrates that day trading is not something you can do while at work or while going out to play golf. You must take an active role in the markets in order to make it work on a systematic basis. Sure, you could buy some stock before heading to the office, and maybe you get lucky and check at lunch and the price is higher so you can sell at a profit. But often, the price may have gone up into a profitable range and may have either dropped down so your profit is a lot less than what it could have been or you're even in a losing position. Scalping isn't very complicated, but it does require that you stay on top of the markets to increase your odds of success and to maximize your success if it does arrive.

Scalping is a pretty basic concept, and that isn't really day trading (although you can certainly do it). Day trading involves planning ahead using well thought out strategies. The first strategy that we'll look at involves using pivot points.

Daily Pivot

The stock market is very volatile, in some sense being guided by chaotic randomness as prices rise and fall at the whims of large numbers of buyers and sellers. Of course, the volatility isn't entirely random, and over the long-term, it gets smoothed out. However, the day trader attempts to take short term advantage of that volatility.

Daily pivot is a strategy that centers on buying your shares at the low point of the day and then (hopefully) selling them at the high point of the day. This strategy does involve a bit of guesswork, there is really no way to know with any certainty what the low and high points of the day are going to be ahead of time – so there is a strong possibility that you will guess wrong.

Of course, we don't want to trade based on a "guess", we're going to use a strategy based on facts (it still may be right or wrong, but we rely on real data to make our trading decisions). This idea is based on the fact that most of the time when dealing with short term movements of stocks, trading is going to proceed based in some part on what the shares have done in the very recent past.

So you calculate what's called a pivot point. This has three inputs: the previous day's high, low, and close. The pivot point is simply the average of the thee:

Pivot point = (high + low + close)/3

Now suppose that we have stock for XYZ. The high, low, and close the previous day were $102, $97, and $100. The pivot point is then:

Pivot point = ($102 + $97 + $100)/3 = $99.67

Now to figure out how to proceed with our trades the following day, we will calculate some support points and points. We will explain what the means in a moment, but first let's learn how to calculate the support points.

Support point 1 = (pivot point x 2) − high from the previous day

Support point 2 = Pivot point − (high − low)

Our support points in this case would be:

S1 = ($99.67 x 2) - $102 = $97.33

S2 = ($99.67) – (102 - $97) = $94.67

Next, we need two resistance points. The formulas used for these are:

R1 = (pivot point x 2) – low from previous day

R2 = Pivot Point + (high – low)

For our example the resistance points are:

R1 = ($99.67 x 2) - $97 = $102.34

R2 = $99.67 + ($102 - $97) = $104.67

We see that the resistance points are above the pivot point, with R1 being a little bit above, and R2 being the most above the pivot point. The support points are below the pivot point, with S1 being a little bit below, and S2 being the lowest point. The numbers R1, R2, S1, S2, and P are only valid for one trading day. Each trading day you need to calculate them using the previous days trading data, prior to the stock market open. You can find pivot point trading calculators on Google.

Stop loss points

A stop loss is a point that is chosen as a kind of insurance to limit losses incurred on security. This is done with a stop-loss order. What you do is you place an order with the broker to buy or sell the stock when it reaches a certain price. As an example, suppose you buy XYZ stock at $100. After you purchase the shares, you can place a stop-loss order for $95. What this does is your shares will be sold if the price drops to $95. That protects you from incurring even more losses if the stock is tanking.

The buy signal

The point of doing these calculations is to determine when to buy, when to sell, and when to cut your losses. The buy signal occurs when the price of the stock goes above the pivot point with conviction. You are bullish on the stock, expecting the price to keep rising (it may not). Your first profit target is given by R1.

By conviction, that means that the stock price is moving up fast. The volume also figures in when evaluating conviction, more volume means more conviction. If there are a lot of volumes and the price is moving up fast, that means more buyers are bullish on the stock.

For our case, the pivot point was $99.67. If the price breaks strongly above this, we take that as a buy signal. The previous days close was $100 so we will say for this example that the share price jumped to $101. We could decide to buy the shares at this price.

The profit point is R1, which is $102.34 based on our calculations. You could choose to sell if the stock price hits R1. However, if the stock is rising rapidly, then you can choose R2 as your profit target. In that case, you would wait until the price hits $104.67 to sell.

If you are right, then you purchased shares of XYZ stock at $101 per share. If we buy 100 shares, then we are in for:

100 x $101 = $10,100

Now suppose that it does hit R2. We immediately sell, so our gross revenue is:

100 x $104.67 = $10,467

We've made a profit of $10,467 - $10,100 = $367. If that was the only trade, we made that day, then we've made a pretty nice daily income of $367.

Of course, things don't always go as planned, which is why you need a stop loss point. You do this so that you can minimize losses and avoid losing your shirt. Whether you stick to R1 or R2 as the point at which you'll sell for a profit or not will depend on how rapidly the stock is going up. So, you'll be looking at a measure of its momentum. The stop loss points S1 and S2 correspond to each case. For R1, which is $102.34, your stop loss point would be S1 = $97.33. If the stock is shooting up and immediately goes above R1, you can take P as your stop loss. If it has gone up to R1 but doesn't show more conviction (i.e. that it's going to go up to R2) then you sell at about R1 and take the smaller profits.

When to use pivot points

There is no solid agreement on this. Some traders believe that pivot points are at their highest accuracy right after the market opens, and so they believe you should utilize them within the first hour of trading. Others believe that the first half-hour of the trading day will have too much volatility, so you should wait before using them.

Opening Range Breakouts

Another day trading strategy is opening range breakouts. The opening range is the first half-hour of the trading day. For the opening range, you mark down the low of the first half-hour and the high of the first half-hour. Suppose that XYZ opens at $90, and then the low of the first half-hour is $89, and the high of the first half-hour is $91. Then the opening range is the difference, or $2. What you'll be looking for is for a breakout, meaning that the stock price either rises with conviction above the high point of the opening range or drops below the low point of the opening range.

If the stock begins to go above the high of the opening range with conviction you can buy the stock, in anticipation that it will continue to increase the rest of the day or most of the rest of the day.

Fading

Fading is a bet against dumb money in the stock market. The technique is based on shorting stocks that have moved upward rapidly, typically in the first hour after market open. The idea is based on the belief that the stock is overbought, that is retail investors have jumped in on stock and bid up to the price based on some news about the stock. During the process, eager retail investors will bid the price up beyond its intrinsic value, so as the trading day goes on the price will begin dropping.

The point to get in and short the stock is to look for when the upswing begins slowing down or fading. Obviously, fading is a high-risk strategy, you don't have the same information available as the institutional investors so may be guessing wrong even when it appears that the rise of the stock is sputtering. You should always protect yourself with a stop-loss.

Candlesticks

A candlestick is a marking on a stock chart or graph that represents the following four data points:

Open

High

Low

Close

Candlesticks are colored red or green on a chart. Just for the sake of seeing a representation, here is a screenshot of a couple of candlesticks for a specific stock:

Candlesticks can be green or red in color. The rectangle shown on the chart is the body of the candlestick. If the candlestick is green, the bottom represents the opening price, and the top represents the closing price. The narrow lines emanating from the candlestick body are called the wicks. If the candlestick is green color, that means the price of the stock went up over the given time period. If you have a monthly chart, then the green color indicates that by the close of the day, for that day the stock went up in price.

A red candlestick indicates that the price of the stock went up for the period of measurement. If the time period is one month, then the top indicates the opening price, while the bottom of the body indicates the opening price.

Different time periods can be illustrated on a graph. In many cases, we are interested in short term price changes for day trading. We can look at a chart that shows whether the price went up or down over a five-minute period. If the price went up over the five-minute periods, the candlestick is green in color. The top of the candlestick body indicates the price at the end of the five-minute period. The bottom indicates the price at the start of the five-minute period.

On the other hand, if the candlestick is colored red, over the given five-minute period, the top represents the price at the start of the five minute period, while the bottom of the body represents the price at the end of the vie minute period.

Let's illustrate this with pictures. Here is the candlestick when it is red in color on the chart:

For a green candlestick, the chart representation is the opposite:

While the top and bottom of the body represent the open and close, the wicks are used to represent the high price, and the low price, respectively.

The top of the candlestick wick represents the high stock price for the day. The bottom of the wick represents the low price of the stock for the day. Or, if the time period is for one day, the ranges represent the change in price over five-minute intervals. So close is the price of the stock at the end of the five-minute period, while open is the price of the stock at the beginning of the five minute period.

Most often, when it comes to day trading, you're going to be looking at trading intervals for one single day so the prices represented will tell you how the stock moved over five-minute intervals:

The high price of the stock over the five-minute interval.

The low price of the stock over the five-minute interval.

The closing or end price at the end of the five-minute interval.

The opening or starting price of the stock over the five-minute interval.

When looking at candlestick charts, you're interested in knowing whether a bearish or bullish engulfing pattern presents itself. So, you pick a candlestick somewhere in the chart and compare that candlestick to the one to the left of the selected candlestick.

If the candlestick on the right side is red and it engulfs or covers the entire range of the candlestick immediately to the left which is green (that is, the trading period five minutes prior), that is a bearish candlestick pattern. Remember that green means the price of the stock went up over the period. If the price goes down over the subsequent period (indicated by red color), then this is a bearish candlestick. If this occurs at the top of an uptrend, then this is considered a reversal candle.

A bullish engulfing or candlestick pattern occurs when you see a red candlestick pattern followed by a green candlestick pattern which engulfs or encompasses the previous candlestick. If a red candlestick is followed by a larger green candlestick at the bottom of a downtrend, then this is considered to be an indication of a reversal.

Here, we have red followed by green at the bottom of a downturn. The green candlestick to the right, which completely covers the red candlestick to the left, is said to engulf the red candlestick. If you are long, this is a good sign. This indicates a reversal, so the stock price can be expected to increase.

On the other hand, suppose we have a red candle that engulfs a green candle. The red is to the right:

If you are shorting a stock, this is a good sign. Otherwise, it's a bad sign. This indicates a reversal if you are at the top of an upturn. That is, the larger red candle which engulfs the green candle to the left (i.e. earlier in time) indicates that the stock is in reversal, which means that the stock is heading to a downturn. If you are long on the stock, it's a bad sign. If you are shorting the stock, or invested in puts, that means that it's a good sign, i.e. that the stock can be expected to be heading into a downturn.

If you see several red candles heading down in a downturn, and then you see a green candle that engulfs the previous red candle, this is bullish – so may indicate a coming upturn on the stock price. So if you are bullish on the stock, this indicates a buying opportunity if you are long, or if you want to buy calls.

If you see several green candles going up, and then there is a red candle the engulfs the previous (to the left) green candle, then this is bearish, that is we expect a downturn in the stock price. If you are buying puts, this is the time to buy.

These are guidelines, but not rules. So, while it might be accurate, it's not going to be accurate all the time.

A shooting star or "inverted hammer" is a candlestick with the top wick much longer than the bottom wick.

The body is small, meaning that the opening and closing price for the time period is not much different. The long wick indicates that the price went up a lot over the period and then closed close to the opening price. A shooting star at the top of an uptrend is considered bearish. It indicates a coming downtrend, which would be bearish if you are long, but good if you want to buy puts.

If this occurs at the bottom of a downtrend, it's an inverted hammer. That is bullish, indicating the stock price should be going up.

These are reversal candles, so are important to recognize in charts. In the chart below, notice that the candle has little or no wick below it, and it has a small body with a long wick above. The candle is red in color. This indicates that it is a bearish candle. This is a sell signal if you are long in the stock, or if you are looking to short, that is a buy signal.

Trading Strategies: Moving Averages

n this chapter, we are going to be taking a deeper look at the concept of moving averages and how they can be used to track the trends in options trading.

It should be noted that the use of moving average as part of technical analysis in options trading is not about tracking the price of options themselves, but the trends in the price of the underlying asset.

Consequently, it is important for you to keep track of the trend seen in the stocks, as well as other assets that you are trading as it is the assets that will determine the prices that will trigger your options contracts.

As such, keep in mind that options trading is not so much about the options contract itself, but rather the trade for the underlying asset that will happen when the triggers points are met on the contract (price and/or maturity).

Based on that, the use of the various types of the moving average will help you visualize where the price of the asset is headed and how you can cash in on the trends. In addition, bear in mind that your assessment of where the trends are headed will determine the overall price points at which you will have to set your options in order to turn a profit.

Definition of moving averages

In essence, a moving average works like any other average. It is the average of the high and low price of an asset over a given period of time.

That is pretty much it. However, it does get a bit more complicated than that.

The average price of an asset over a given period of time is a static measure that simply reflects the buy and sell price of the asset in a rather specific window of time. It is a snapshot, if you will, of what that asset's price has been over a longer period of time.

As such, a moving average becomes the calculation of the average price of an asset at given intervals, for instance, every hour. With this calculation on a recurring basis, the asset's price can be tracked to determine where the trend, if any, lies.

The various results of the moving average calculation can be plotted on a chart in which each point can be used to determine the overall trend of the asset's price. There are three possible types of trends:

Upward trend. This type of trend indicates that the overall trend in the price of an asset is up, meaning, increase. It is very important to keep in mind that an upward trend is generally accompanied by higher demand though it is not always the case. Nevertheless, increased demand generally means an increase in price.

Downward trend. This type of trend indicates that the overall trend in the price of an asset down, meaning decrease. What this indicates in that the price is going down as a result of an increase of supply, or a decrease in demand. Both forces can converge thus leading the asset's prices to spiral downward.

Sideways trend. In this case, there is little to no change in the price of the asset. This means that the trend remains steady. When this happens, it is because investors are being cautious. Perhaps they are expecting a breakout. So, while the breakout happens, they are holding their positions in order to see that will transpire.

Additionally, moving averages use a statistical technique called "candlesticks" to track the high and low price of the asset at every interval the price is measured. In this regard, you can visualize the amount of volatility as reflected in the fluctuations of the asset's price. Consequently, you can gain a great deal of perspective as to what the sentiment of investors is with regard to the asset in question.

Uses of moving averages

The main function of a moving average is to track the trend in the price of an asset.

It is the premier tool used by traders and analysts in order to gauge the sentiment of investors. If investors are piling on to an asset, you will see this reflected in the price of the asset. On the contrary, if investors are looking to dump an asset, the moving average will reflect this sentiment.

This is why you, as a day trader, need to recognize these trends. The most important thing to keep in mind is that depending on your overall trading approach, you will be able to figure out what the best play for you is.

Given the fact that the moving average reflects very short-term moves, in addition to longer-term moves, you can figure out if the asset in question is good for a short-term trade, or perhaps it might be better suited for a long-term approach.

For instance, if you see a high degree of volatility, then you might figure that the asset would potentially payoff big time as part of your day trading strategy.

On the other hand, if you see that there is little movement in the stock due to the fact that it is trading in a very narrow range, then you might be looking at a stock which is poised to breakout. This is a very important consideration as the moving average then serves a speculative purpose.

Moving averages, when available, can serve to view the price of stocks over a very long period of time, such as several years. This is a powerful analytics tool as you can see what the performance of the stock has been over a much more extended period of time. Consequently, you can choose to hold on to it as part of a passive income strategy or as a means of hedging your portfolio against riskier propositions.

So, I would greatly encourage you to become familiar with moving averages as this will be the basic parameter by which you will be able to measure the performance of stocks, and any other asset, you wish to trade.

The various types of moving averages

In the study of moving averages, you will find several types which are commonly tracked by traders They are as follows:

The two-day moving average

The ten-day moving average

The fifty-day moving average

The two hundred-day moving average

While moving averages could conceivably be tracked over any period, the above-mentioned moving averages are tracked as part of an industry-wide practice.

If you look at most data and analytics subscriptions, you will find data going back to at least five years on the vast majority of stocks. You can find data on some going back to as much as 30 years, though you won't be getting moving average data, but something more like monthly data throughout such period of time.

Surely, being able to have as much data a possible will help you make wise investment decisions. Although, taking a deep look at the time periods described above will help you follow the same patterns that other investors are looking at.

So, let's begin with the two-day average.

The two-day average tracks the movement of the price of an asset, generally hour by hour. This will allow you to see what kind of fluctuation and/or volatility there might be in the price of an asset. This is the most commonly used type of moving average. It is the best measure which can be used by a day trader especially if you are looking to cash out at the end of each trading day. This average is also the basis for placing options at the beginning of your trading day.

The ten-day average is used to measure short-term investments. This is a good measure for swing traders to use, as well as, day trader. A swing trader basically does the same as a day trader except that they won't cash out at the end of each trading day. They may leave positions open for much longer than a single day. They generally close all of their positions out by Friday evening. Therefore, they may hold on to a position for several days. This is why the ten-day average is very useful. In addition, the ten-day average is a good measure for determining if the trend observed over a two-day period is consistent or if it is an outlier when compared to the overall trend of the stock.

The fifty-day average covers a period of almost two months. In this average, investors can get a very good feel for the trend of the stock. Given that it will have hourly data over the course of fifty days, you can certainly imagine that the information visualized over this period of time will serve investors well in making a fair assessment as to the direction an asset is headed.

The two hundred-day average is the longest measure of time. While it is still quite a few days short of a year, experience and practice have shown that two hundred days is enough time to establish a very good idea of the patterns being observed. Furthermore, investors can contrast the two hundred-day moving average to the fifty-day average and determine if the stock is heading straight on the same path, or if there might be a reversal headed.

As such, it is important to recognize if a reversal in trend is on the horizon as reversals can refer to either an upward trend heading down or a downward trend heading up. Also, if a stock is trading sideways, you might be poised to see a breakout coming, or perhaps the bottom falling out of the stock.

Either way, it is certainly worth keeping an eye on all of the various types of moving averages so that you can make an informed decision before plunging in headlong into an investment.

Using moving averages in day trading

As mentioned earlier, the ideal measure for day traders is the two-day average.

Why?

Well, day trading, by definition, is the shortest-term type of trading. In fact, you might hear stories of folks who have made $1,000 profit in ten seconds. That's how short day trading is.

Consequently, you need to be on your heels and make sure that you can see where the trend is going. Perhaps you have noticed a stock trading in a given range, and then you see it dipping a bit. So, this might be the time to buy on the dip and then sell once the stock picks up again.

Also, identifying these patterns in the two-day average can help you predict potential price points. Therefore, you can set up your options and sit back to watch the action unfold.

The downside to using moving averages is that it does require a bit of observation and research. While this information might be at the tip of your fingers, you do need to keep an eye on it at all times. This will ensure that you don't fall asleep at the wheel.

Now, looking at the other types of moving averages can help you figure out if what you are seeing in the two-day average is consistent. If it isn't, then you need to ask yourself what's going on. Perhaps it is just a knee-jerk reaction by investors to some other exogenous factors which are not related to the stock itself but do have a bearing on it.

In addition, keeping an eye on the two hundred-day average is a great way for you to plan several moves ahead. Perhaps you can identify a potential breakout or reversal. If you can visualize, then it will help you play several moves ahead. So, when you see the breakout coming, you will be ready to pounce on the opportunity and make the deal happen.

So, I would encourage you to make the study of moving averages your bread and butter as a day trader. This is especially important if you decide to branch out and hold your positions open longer than you normally would. That way, you can gain a better sense of where the market is headed, and what direction the stock will take.

Based on this, you can make informed decisions about your trades. Just one final thought: always double check information. So, if you can rely on a free data and analytics account and the contrast that with a premium account, you will be able to determine if the information you are seeing is accurate.

Now, that is not to say that these companies might be purposely reporting inaccurate information, but some of the free services might be operating on a lag; hence, the free part.

Thus, if you can spend a couple of bucks, then definitely consider it. It should pay off in the long run big time.

Chapter 4 Step by Step to a successful trade

When it comes to selecting brokers, you have many options available. There are full service, discount, online, etc. Understanding the differences between them and selecting the ones best suited for your purposes is crucial if you wish to succeed. Another area that a lot of beginners ignore and then receive a rude lesson in is the regulations surrounding options trading.

There aren't too many rules to comply with, but they do have significant consequences for your capital and risk strategies. This chapter is going to fill you in on all the details.

What broker to use?

Generally speaking, there are two major varieties of brokers: Discount and full service. In fact, a lot of full-service brokers have discount arms these days so you will see some overlap. Full service refers to an organization where brokerage is just a part of a larger financial supermarket.

The broker might offer you other investment solutions, estate planning strategies, and so on. They'll also have an in house research wing which will send you reports to help you trade better. In addition to this, they'll also have phone support in case you have any questions or wish to place an order.

Once you develop a good relationship with them, a full-service broker will become a good organization to network. Every broker loves a profitable customer since it helps with marketing. A full-service broker will have good relationships in the industry and if you have specific needs, they can put you in touch with the right people.

The price of all this service is you paying higher commissions than average. It is up to you to see whether this is a good price for you to pay. As such, you don't need to signup with a full-service broker to trade successfully. Order matching is done electronically so it's not as if a person on the floor can get you a better price these days. Therefore, a full-service house is not going to give you better execution.

Discount brokers, on the other hand, are all about focus. They help you trade, and that is it. They will not provide advice, at least not intentionally from a business perspective, and phone ordering is nonexistent. That doesn't mean customer service is reduced. Far from it.

Commissions will be lower as well, far lower than what you can expect to pay at a full-service house. The downside of a discount brokerage is that you're not going to receive any special product recommendations or solutions outside of your speculative activities. A lot of people prefer to trade (using a separate account) with the broker they have their retirement accounts with so everything is kept in-house.

So which one should you choose? Well, if you aim to keep costs as low as possible, then select a discount broker. In fact, only in the case where you're keen on keeping things in one place should you choose a full-service broker. These days, there's no difference between the two options otherwise.

An exception here is if you have a large amount of capital, north of half a million dollars. In such cases, a full-service broker will be cheaper because of their volume-based commission offers. You'll pay the same rate or as close to what a discount broker would charge you, and you get all the additional services. Whatever additional amounts you need to invest can be handled by the firm through their wealth management line of business.

There are a few terms you must understand, no matter which broker you choose so let's look at these now.

Margin

Margin refers to the number of assets you currently hold in your account. Your assets are cash and positions. As the market value of your positions fluctuates, so does the amount of margin you have. Margin is an important concept to grasp since it is at the core of your risk management discipline.

When you open an account with your broker, you will have a choice to make. You can open either a cash or margin account. In order to trade options, you have to open a margin account. Briefly, a cash account does not include leverage within it, so all you can trade are stocks. There are no account minimums for a cash account, and even if they are, they're pretty minuscule.

A margin account, on the other hand, is subject to very different rules. First, the minimum balances for a margin account are higher. Most brokers will impose a $10,000 minimum, and some will even increase this amount based on your trading style. The account minimum doesn't achieve anything by itself, but it acts as a commitment of sorts for the broker.

The thinking is that with this much money on the line, the person trading is going to be a bit more serious about it and won't blow it away. If only it worked like that. Anyway, the minimum balance is a hard and fast rule. Another rule you should be aware of is the Pattern Day Trader (PDT) designation.

PDT is a rule that comes directly from the SEC. Anyone who executes four or more orders within five days is classified as a PDT ("Pattern Day Trader," 2019). One this tag is slapped onto you, your broker is going to ask you to post at least $25,000 in the margin as a minimum balance. Again, this minimum balance doesn't do anything but the SEC figures that if you do screw up, this gives you enough of a buffer.

Will the strategies in this book get you classified as a PDT? Well, this depends on you. Each strategy by itself plays out over a month or more so once you enter, all you need to do is monitor it and if you want, you can adjust it. However, if you're going to avoid the PDT, you're limited to entering just three positions per workweek.

My advice is to study the strategies and to start slowly. Trade just one instrument at first and see how it goes and then expand once you gain more confidence. At that point, you'll have enough experience to figure out how much capital you need. Remember that even exiting a position is considered a trade, so PDT doesn't refer just to trade entry.

Building up your Watch list

One other aspect of margin you must understand is the margin call. This is a dreaded message for most traders, including institutional ones. The purpose of all risk management is to keep you as far away as possible from this ever happening to you. A margin call is issued when you have inadequate funds in your account to cover its requirements.

Remember that your margin is the combination of the cash you hold plus the value of your positions. If you have $1000 in cash, but your position is currently in a loss of -$900, you'll receive a margin call to post more cash to cover the potential loss you're headed for. In fact, you'll receive it well in advance. If you don't post more margin, your broker has the right to close out your positions and recover whatever cash they can to stop their risk limits from being triggered.

The threshold beyond which your broker will issue a margin call is called the maintenance margin. Usually, you need to maintain 25% of your initial position value (that is when you enter a position) as cash in your account. Most brokers have a handy indicator which tells you how close you are to the limit.

The leading cause of margin calls is leverage. With a margin account, you can borrow money from your broker and use that to boost your returns. Let's look at an example: if you trade with $10,000 of your own money and borrow $20,000 from your broker to enter a position, you control $30,000 worth of the position. Let's say this position makes a gain of $10,000 to bring its total value to $40,000.

You've just made a 100% return on this investment (since you invested just $10,000) despite the total return on the position is 33% (10,000/30,000). What happens if you lose $10,000 on the position though? Well, you just lost 100% despite the position losing only 33%. Leverage is a double-edged sword.

It is far too simplistic to call leverage bad or good. It is what it is. If you're a beginner, you should not be borrowing money to trade under any circumstances. When you're experienced, you can choose to do so as much as you want. Please note, I'm differentiating between the leverage where you borrow money, and the sort of leverage options provide.

With options, a single contract gives you control over a larger pie of stock, but the option premium still needs to be paid. It is, therefore, cheaper to trade options than the common stock. If you were to borrow money to pay for the option premium, then you're indulging in foolish behavior, and you need to step away.

There's a difference between leverage being inherent within the structure of the instrument and using leverage to increase the amount of something you can buy. The latter should be avoided when you're a beginner.

Execution

A favorite pastime of unsuccessful traders is to complain about execution. Their losses are always the broker's fault, and if it weren't for the greedy brokers, they'd be rolling in the dough, diving in and out of it like Scrooge McDuck. Complaining about your execution will get you nothing. A big reason for these complaints is that most beginner traders don't realize that the price they see on the screen is not the same as what is being traded on the exchange.

We live in an era of high-frequency trading, and the markets' smallest measurement of time has gone from seconds to microseconds. Trades are constantly pouring in, and the matching engine is always finding suitable sellers for buyers. Given the pace of the market, it is important to understand that it is humanly impossible to figure out the exact price of an instrument.

Therefore, within your risk management plan, you must make allowance for times of high volatility when the fluctuations will be bigger. For now, I want you to understand that just because the price you received was different from what was on screen doesn't mean the broker is incompetent.

How do you identify an incompetent broker? Customer service and the quality of the trading terminal they give you access to are the best indicators. Your broker is not in the game to trade against you or fleece you. Admittedly, this is not the case with FX, but we're not discussing FX in this book. So stop blaming your broker and look at your systems instead, assuming the broker passes basic due diligence.

When it comes to placing orders with your broker, you have many options. There are different order types you can place, and each order has a specific purpose. First off, we have the market order. This is the simplest order to understand. When you place a market order, you're telling your broker to fill your entire order at whatever price they can find on the market.

A market order usually results in fast fills, unless there's a volatility event of some sort going on. The next type of order you can place is the limit order. The limit prioritizes order price over quantity. For example, if you want to enter 100 units of an instrument at $10, your broker will buy as much as possible under or equal to $10. If they can get just 90 units under $10, then that's it.

A limit order works for a lot of traders looking to enter a position. Directional risk management depends a lot on the size of the position, so it is critical not to exceed the positions limit. For such traders, this is a beneficial order. The last type of order you will encounter is the stop order. The stop prioritizes quantity over price.

Stop orders have a trigger attached to them, and once market price hits the trigger, the entire quantity of the order is executed, irrespective of what the price is. Stop orders are very useful to get out of positions quickly. Indeed, the stop-loss order is a stop order with the 'loss' in the name simply referring to the minimization of losses in case the trade goes south.

Another order you should be aware of is the Good Till Cancelled or GTC. A cousin of the GTC is the Day order. These two do not order types as much as expiry conditions for the order. A GTC is valid until the trader explicitly cancels it while the day order cancels itself at the end of the market session.

All in all, there are over a hundred different types of order your average broker offers you. Do not get bogged down trying to figure them all out. Institutional traders use most of them for specific strategies. To trade well, you don't need to understand a single word of what those orders are about. Stick to the ones mentioned here, and you can trade successfully.

The question now is, how and where should you use these orders? Well since you're trading options, you're not going to be too concerned with stop losses and your exits are going to involve letting options expire. Thus, the biggest concern you should have is with regard to trade entry.

With options, you can choose either market or limit orders to enter. Personally, I favor market orders since it guarantees you an entry. Risk management here is a bit different than with directional trades so you can afford to enter at the market. The only exception is if there are extreme volatility conditions present.

Trading Plan (entry, exit, and stop loss)

A lot of traders are stumped when they first look at their trading screens and see that there are two prices for everything. After all, every financial channel always displays one price for security but when trading, you'll be quoted two different prices within the price box. This is a small but crucial detail for you to understand.

The lower price you receive is called the bid, and this is the price you will pay if you sell the instrument. The higher price is the ask, and this is what you will pay to buy the instrument. The single price you see on your TV screen is the "Last Traded Price" or LTP. Do not make the mistake of thinking the LTP is the real price since the market moves constantly.

In fact, even the spread (the difference between the ask and the bid) doesn't accurately reflect the true state of things thanks to constant movement. There's no need to be alarmed though, as long as volatility is stable, the difference isn't much. Just remember to look at the spread to understand what you'll be paying. The spread increases and contracts constantly but if you see that it is getting too big, this is a sign that too much volatility exists and you're better off staying out.

This concludes our look at brokers and the ins and outs of it. As you can see, there isn't too much to be concerned about, but you need to be well aware since it impacts how much capital you'll be trading with. Generally speaking, the higher the capital you have, the safer you'll be since you'll have more room to make mistakes.

Being undercapitalized is one of the biggest reasons traders fail in the markets, so don't make the mistake of jumping in too soon. Also, don't try to get creative with the PDT to the detriment of your strategy. There are several gurus online who will give you 'tricks' and 'hacks' to get by this but resist the temptation.

Lastly, I've mentioned this in passing before but don't be the person who rings up their broker for investment advice. I mean, even Hollywood has figured out that this is a bad idea and has innumerable movies for you to learn from.

Your approach to trading determines how well you'll manage your risk. The real key to trading success is risk management and the simple math that underlines it. We'll look at this next.

Chapter 5 Introduction
to candlesticks

Now that you have a sound idea of what the best day trading techniques are, you can begin to strategize so that you can make a substantial reward from all of your efforts. The ultimate goal for any day trader is to make a sizeable profit, and in order to fulfill this goal, it is necessary to control a big amount of capital.

Day traders understand that when working towards making this profit, speed and timing are everything. This is because they are focused on finding and making use of the minutest movements in stocks which have high liquidity or index. Without the right strategy, they are unlikely to succeed. A retail day trader can try out the following strategies: -

Price action and Mass psychology
It is not every stock on the market that is suitable for a day trader. There are certain criteria that make some stocks more viable than others. A day trader will evaluate a stock based on two variables. The first is the liquidity of the stock. This primarily looks at the pricing of the stock, and the ease with which a trader can enter

or exit this stock. The best stock for day trading will have a tight spread, as well as a low spillage.

The second variable that a day trader will evaluate is the volatility of a stock. The mention of volatility explains movement, and in day trading, it refers to the movement in price. When evaluating volatility, the day trader takes into consideration the price range that is expected for the day. This could have two significant results; it could lead to heightened profits or significant losses.

Once liquidity and volatility have been assessed, and the stock has been identified as being appropriate for trading, the next step is to look into the best way to identify entry points. For this, there are two tools that come in handy.

Bullish candlesticks

These charts are highly popular and are essential for any day trader. They display the prices for specific securities on a daily basis. By analyzing a candlestick chart, it is possible to know the day's highest and lowest prices, as well as the opening and closing price.

In addition to this, the shape of the candle in the candlestick chart reveals more information. The section which is wide is referred to as the 'real body'. It is within this section that one can analyze the closing price in relation to the opening price, by assessing whether it was higher or lower. This is denoted by specific colors. When the stock closes at a price that is lower, the candle will be black or red in color. However, when it closes at a price that is higher, the candle will be white or green in color.

The shadow of the candle in this chart also tells a story. It explains the highs and lows for the day, and this can then be compared to the opening and closing prices. So in the final analysis, just the shape of the candle will vary based on all the movements taking place in a day's trade. This type of chart provides a straightforward analysis of pricing for the day.

Bearish candlesticks

When a gambler goes to the races, they receive a thrill by watching everything unfolding live, right before their eyes. There is an equivalent for this in day trading, and this is referred to as Level II. A trader who is using this strategy is watching the trades being executed live, right before their eyes. This is based on quotes from specific market makers. As everything unfolds, rapid decisions can be made to ensure that any small gain is capitalized on – in real time.

ECN stands for Electronic Communication Network. This is an automated system which allows traders from different locations to trade with each other easily. It works by matching buy and sell orders. This system is great for a day trader who operates as an individual because by using an ECN, the trader can actually connect directly with a major brokerage. This cuts down on fees for a middleman, and also saves time, allowing for faster and more profitable trades. The added advantage of an ECN is that trading extends beyond the typical market hours, and includes after-hours trading.

In addition to these two tools, there is a chart that can prove handy when reading information for data trading. Simply being able to understand the information that is available can go a long way in creating a foundation for success.

Discerning the information from day trading transactions would be a challenge if there was no mechanism in place to make it possible. All the information from day trading is arranged in different types of trading charts. By using these trading charts, a day trader is able to keep an eye on the markets that they are trading on, and this makes it easier to make informed decisions about when they should be making their trades. It also allows them to monitor the movements on the market on a consistent basis.

There is a range of different trading charts that are available. These trading charts will all provide you with similar information, and that includes the prices that are currently being traded. Of all the available options, there are three which are referred to with heightened regularity. Candlestick charts have been discussed above. The other two are explained in this section.

Candlestick charts were said to have come into existence a hundred years ago in Japan before the developed world created the bar charts, as well as point-and-figure charts.

Homma, a Japanese man in the seventeen century was said to find out there was a relationship between the demand and supply of rice, as well as its price. It was said the markets were controlled a lot by how the traders felt.

Candlesticks end up displaying the emotion by representing physically the amount of price movements using varying hues.

Traders tend to utilize candlesticks when they want to reach trading decisions. This is usually dependent on those patterns that are always occurring, allowing one to forecast where the price direction would be in the short term.

Components of Candle Sticks

A daily candlestick bears similarity to a bar chart, being that it displays the daily low, high, as well as the close price of the market.

The candlestick usually possesses a great aspect that makes up what is christened as the "real body."

The real body is that part that acts as the range of price between the closing and opening of a day's trading session.

If you see that the real body has either the black hue or is filled up, then it means that the closing position ended up being lower when compared to the opening position.

If you see that the real body came out empty, then the opening position was lower than the closing one.

Traders can change the hues in their trading platform. If you see a down candle, there is a great chance that it would be painted red, and not black. For the up candles, they could be painted green, and not white.

Traders use candlestick charts to find out probable movement in prices depending on previous patterns.

When you are trading in any market for that matter, candlesticks are awesome because they display the four price points, which are low, high, closed and open, in that time that the trader wishes for.

A lot of algorithms function with similar price details seen in candlestick charts. Usually, trading is affected by emotions, and this can be seen in a candlestick chart.

How to Read a Candlestick Chart

A lot of traders can't get over the usage of candlestick charts since they offer a large number of details, as well as a design that ensures that you can easily read it, and understand it without stress.

This chart got its name as a result of the indicators or markers, the fact that it has a body that reminds one of a candle, as well as a line showing on the top, which bears a resemblance to a wick. This line is called a tail or shadow. Candlesticks also tend to possess a tail or shadow on the end.

When you look at the chart, you will notice that every candlestick has a low, high, open and close price for that period the trader wants.

If a trader decides to put the period at five minutes, this means a brand new candlestick forms at every five minutes. This works well in an intraday chart.

That's not all candlesticks do, as they can display the price that is showing. You will see the following there:

Open price

If you look at the candle body's bottom or top, you will see the open price. This is dependent on if the asset is swinging lower or higher in the five-minute period.

If you notice that the price is moving up, then the candlestick is either white or green, while the open price is situated very low.

If you notice that the price is moving in a downward direction, then the candlestick is either black or red. You will also see that the open price is at the peak.

High price

If high price occurs in the candlestick period, then you will see it at the shadow's top or on the tail on top of the body. You won't see any upper shadow, if the close or open ended up being the largest price.

Low price

This low is shown by the shadow's bottom or on the tail underneath the body. You won't see any lower shadow if the close or open ended up being the lowest price.

Close price

That price that ends up the trade in a candlestick is seen as the close. The top shows it if the candle is white or green. If the candle is black or red, then it is seen at the bottom of the body.

When a candle occurs, it tends to be altered once the price changes. Usually, the open doesn't change, but the low and high prices will continue to be altered as long as the candle hasn't been completed.

The hue may be altered too while the candlestick develops. The candlestick may change from the greenish hue to the reddish one, if its recent price was once on top of the open price, but ended up falling underneath it.

If the candle's period ends, the price that ends it is the closer price, meaning that the candle has ended. A new one will be developed.

Price direction

When you look at the candlestick chart, it is easy to see where the price moved to while the candle was still in existence by looking at the position and hue of the candlestick.

If you notice that the candlestick has the greenish hue, the closing price occurred on top of where the opening price was. This candle will be seen on top and the right corner of the prior one, except it comes off as having a different hue or being shorter than the prior candle.

You can tell that the closing price was underneath where the opening price is, if the Candlestick has the reddish hue. This is also reinforced if the candle is situated underneath and on the right side of the prior candle. This is true except when it has a different hue or is shorter than the other candle.

Price range

You can tell what the price range of a Candlestick in a period is by looking at the distance between the lower shadow's bottom and the upper shadow's top.

It is easy to get the range by taking out the low price from the high price. If you want to understand candlestick charts well, you have to create a demo trading account. You can also consider using candlesticks on those free to use web-based charting structures. When you have registered, choose candlestick as your chart type, then click on a time frame of one minute. This allows you to have access to a myriad of candles that can be stared at.

Try and find what every candle means, before you start searching for awesome trading opportunities from the candlestick patterns like three black crows.

The candlestick has different elements.

The First Element: The Body Size

If you want to get a lot of information, you need to look at the candle body because it is the reservoir of knowledge.

When you see a long body, know that it has strength. If you notice that the body is becoming larger, then there is an improvement in momentum.

If you notice that the candle body is now turning smaller, momentum is slowing. With the body, you can tell the way prices has moved throughout the candle.

Second Element: The wicks' length

When you look at the wicks, you can tell how volatile the price movements are.

If the wicks are larger, then the price has moved about a lot of times while the candle was living, but it ended up being rejected.

If the candle wicks end up being larger, it means that there was an improvement in volatility. You will see this when after the appearance of long trending phases, then a reversal occurs. You can also see them at massive resistance and support levels.

The Third Element: The ratio that exists between bodies and wicks.

When you look at the candle, what do you see? Longer bodies or wicks?

When a high momentum trend is happening, long bodies that have tiny wicks will become common.

If the uncertainty level improves, you will see that the volatility will increase, while the bodies end up being tinier. You will also see that the wicks ended up being bigger.

The Fourth Element: The body's position

This acts as the elongation of the prior point. Look at it, do you see a long wick that has a body on the other side?

This normally shows rejection of some sort.

You will notice indecision when the candle has a tiny body in its middle, while having longer wicks.

What is a shadow

The wick or shadow is that line that is seen in a candlestick chart, to show where the stock's price has altered and linked to the closing and opening prices.

Normally, the shadows tend to show the lowest and highest prices at which that stock has been traded in a period.

Earlier on, we said that the wide part of the candlestick is called the real body.

You can see the shadow either under the close or on top of the open.

If you notice a long shadow showing on the candle's bottom, appealing like a hammer, then there may be an increment in the purchase level. It could also mean a bottom based on the pattern.

In trading, there exist two types of analysis, and they are technical and fundamental analysis.

The fundamental analysis is dependent on how the company performs when it wants to provide insights and clues on where the stock is going in the future. Fundamental analysts are known to analyze revenue metrics, as well as earnings.

Technical analysts, on the other hand, tend to focus on price movements. They seek out those patterns in the price action, while making use of these patterns in the prediction of where the price is going to in the future.

When fundamental analysis is done, it helps traders to know what stocks to trade. In the case of technical analysis, it lets you know the perfect time to trade. An example of a technical analysis tool is the candlestick chart.

When some technical analysts see a long or tall shadow, they feel that the stock will soon face a reversal.

Some have the notion that a lower or shorter shadow translates to a price increase coming. If you see a long upper shadow, know that a downturn is about to come. If you notice a long lower shadow, know that rise is on the way.

You will see a long upper shadow if the price starts to move in the time frame, but still reverses down. This is seen as the bear sign.

Bulls tend to increase the price, while bears attempt to drive it down.

If a candlestick doesn't have a shadow, buyers or sellers may see it as a strong signal for something, and that thing is based on where the candle's direction is. This candlestick happens when the price action of security refuses to trade outside the closing and opening prices range.

Chapter 6 Tools and Platforms

A vital aspect of options trading is the platform that one uses to trade. This is because options trading requires monitoring and requires a continuous analysis of trends. Performance is also monitored, and since the trade is impacted upon by a complex of factors, one has to choose a suitable platform for trading.

A good platform for trading should offer a lot of opportunities for traders. These are opportunities to orient beginners into trading, development for the existing ones, and actualization for those with a record on the platform. A platform of trading should also prescribe the available products and any resources that subscribers on the platform can benefit from to push themselves to profitability.

With the technology developing at high speed, platforms continue to improve by the day. This is both complicating the trading itself as well as providing avenues of spreading awareness about the business. A platform should, therefore, have the ability to offer the best possible experience for the traders to do trade and grow both in experience and returns without meeting a lot of platform limitations and frustrations.

A Platform Takes Trading To the Holders

Trading involves a lot of complexities that may sometimes be scary. It makes people lose interest as soon as they develop it. They perceive it as too complicated. The impression is that it is a venture meant for the people who have higher comprehension of concepts in the economics specialty and that those who do not a background in this area will have difficulty getting on board.

However, a trading platform has to present options trading as a venture that is possible and in which anyone with interest can succeed in. The days when options trading and any other forms of trading were presented as a show of sophistication are long gone. In this era, every sector of investment is being portrayed as possible, and businesses are now being made easier in order to create a better chance for people to dare. A platform that limits investment so much and is exclusive in terms of how it carries out its trading activities is irrelevant to modern economic patterns.

Platforms, therefore, have to be interactive and user-friendly. They should have the ability to encourage users to feel like they can handle the trade. It should also have the capability to gauge the level of use and give feedback about how well they are able to use it. If it is a website, for instance, it has to be able to report the numbers as people visit it and how many eventually end up creating accounts and trading. Counting traffic is essential for feedback that can lead to the creation of a better experience for the users.

Competition

The reason for considering a good platform is because the competition is high today. Competition has led to the creation of better trading experiences through innovation. Platforms are now trying to out-do each other in being the avenues of options trading. They are doing this by striving to create ways of improving user experience. It is therefore essential to identify the various parameters of comparing the platforms. Eventually, one has to choose a platform that offers optimal access to the trading world.

In choosing a platform sometimes, one would want to take advantage of the advantages of different platforms. This is looking at one's style of trading and how they wish to monitor their business and see if a platform is more transparent in handling the tares or whether it offers a clear lens of controlling purchases and sells of options. This is the reason why the various platforms have to be assessed in terms of their potential. Usually, platforms are related to the tools of trading. Some of the tools of trading can be found right on the platform of trading.

When a platform of trading also has various tools of aiding trading, it ensures that one can gain a lot of benefits at one place. This makes the platform a utility platform where a person can visit for more purposes than just trading. It also makes it better. For instance, if a platform has videos that offer trading tutorials. This can make it resourceful in imparting competency in participating in the very sector that the platform operates.

To best benefit from competition, one has to understand the type of trade they want to do. This is by naming their price and gauging which platform can serve better in ensuring returns and value generation. This is in order to avoid going into trading in desperation, and one has to be patient to see if the platform can also come out and meet a trader at their point of ability and also help in trading in comfort where risk is at a minimum.

Charting software

There are various platforms in options trading that one could consider. There is web-based trading that utilizes the power of the search engines. This platform has many operators since the building of websites in the modern age is easy. This platform is responsible for the growth in the popularity of options trading. People can trade from anyone, open brokerage accounts, make deposits, and participate in the buying and selling of assets in the comfort of their homes.

With the presence of a lot of technological gadgets such as smartphones, tablets, and computers, web-based trading has been easy and possible. Websites can be built with additional resources for learning and tools that can be an advantage for both novice and seasoned traders. On the websites, regular updates on the market can be posted to keep traders informed about trends, patterns, and even help in analyzing price movements for the subscribers.

The web is also a good platform when it comes to filtering opportunities and options based on suitability and preference in view of the various abilities of users. They can be designed to be customizable even when the options markets are standardized.

User Friendliness

Usually, websites are good as they offer various tools that aid beginners to edge into trading options. ASX, for example, offers a variety of web-based resources that guide people in their efforts to understand trading. This includes online chats that have instant feedback as a team is dedicated to the work site for correspondence purposes. The aim of this is to offer motivation and impetus to go on with the discovery of the markets trends until one becomes a seasoned trader.

Friendliness is also in terms of the efforts that are made to create peer assistance. This is through creating groups of traders that influence each other and can learn from the vast experiences in the trading of the options. This can be a positive influence on the journey to gaining competence and help support an environment where people can relate and interact as they pursue their various financial goals.

It is important to consider the fact that some of the platforms of trading offer important tools that can be helpful in deciding on options. The tools are those that help in monitoring markets and simplify the technical analysis process for the trader. This can help one to sharpen their trading strategy to align well with the ultimate goal of trading. This depends on whether the goal of trading is to earn money in terms of profit or hedge oneself against losses on the underlying asset.

Tools to Learn

Upon mastering the various basics of trading and making the initial moves to start trading, one has to use various tools that help to indicate the advancers and decliners on the market. Greeks are some kind of metrics that those involved in options trading capitalize to ensure maximization of returns. These "Greeks" include the delta matrix that measures the correlation between price movements of the underlying asset relative to the price of the option. The tools for monitoring the movements for these parameters of trading are vital as everyone is always trading with a focus on minimizing losses while geared towards profit maximization.

The gamma is another tool that can help to predict market trends in order to do good timing for decisions on exercising rights in options. Gamma is an indicator of the rate of delta variations for the option price as compared to the asset price. This goes hand in hand with the time-decay tool that indicators the value movement, either upwards or downwards, in the period of life options. This helps to signal which options to avoid given the remaining time of the life span and the value implications thereon.

There is also the aspect of the volatility of the asset underlying a particular option trade. Some of the assets or stocks do not have inherent volatility to appreciate in value due to their nature. Assets that have high market volatility usually gain a lot on the market, and hence, the value behaves better to favor the call option trade. Products with ugh volatility and high inherent value are not suitable for the put option trade since they will occasion a loss. It is therefore important to use correct tools that aid in the analysis if the technical mechanics of the options trading business.

Tools are not just concrete things that can be manipulated. Some tools, especially in trading, are conceptual in nature. This is because they are the ones by which one can trade and aid in decision making. They sample out market forces and help in mapping out market trends for the benefit of the trader. To perceive tools as only concrete in nature is a misconception of the whole options trading venture.

Professional level platforms

There is a level in trading where one attains sophistication and attains the intuition to thrive in options trading regardless of the ways market forces seem to behave. At this level, someone needs tools that can help them edge into the horizon of complexity in trading. The platforms for this professional level exist, and they have to offer tools that are an edge above the basic level. These tools have to offer strategies of competing to control the stocks and rise above the market forces. At this level, one becomes daring, and the possibilities that the platform offers should only be dared by those who have mastered trading and are sure of beating odds as they speculate about squeezing out value form trades that otherwise be perceived as highly risky.

The platform should be full of idea probing resources that lead one to gain the courage to trade more and more. Web-based platforms of this level include the think or swim platform that is categorically for seasoned traders. This is the reason why one has to know the platform to trade on based on their level of experience in options trading. Some platforms are too complicated for the starters. The tools are even out of the capacity of a beginner to comprehend the trades appear to have higher risks that may wipe away hard-earned fortunes.

Mobile Trading

Some platforms have taken advantage of the handiness of the mobile era. These entail the smartphone lifestyle and the flashier iPod, iPad, and tablet culture. This is when trading is being placed in the palms of traders to hold and run away with it. This platform usually targets traders that want to capitalize on device optimization. This is the reason why trades have classes. Some of the options could be device targeted as they can only be taken advantage of when one using the suitable device for trading, provided the relevant support tools that the device offers.

Mobile trading also comes in order to keep people abreast. This is because opportunities sometimes appear and disappear on people because they are not using a device that enables them to be precise and timely in decision making and action.

With mobile trading, apps have been developed, some with notification capability. One can customize the apps to ensure that no opportunity comes that is not taken advantage of. Opportunities' in trading have to be seized and relying on a platform that is less handy and far means that opportunities of trading are lost.

What Are We Looking For In Platforms And Tools?

First is the opportunity to learn. There is no worse platform of trading than that which targets only to admit traders who do not understand what they are getting into. The education that a platform has to offer should be free as trading is itself risky enough to prohibit any extra expenses in the process. Platform operators should understand that any interested person who visits their platform is a potential subscriber, and they should freely offer support to educate them for the purpose of acquisition of requisite knowledge on options trading.

Some of the platforms have gone as opening structures units for education on options trading. These courses are taken online, and coaching is done through the provision of a stream of webinars transmitted live or uploading recorded ones. This is for platforms that appreciate that trading is an informed gamble that requires one to know enough. They even test the proficiency of understanding trading concepts and mechanics for the purpose of ensuring that any people who trade on the platform are doing what they understand to build the platform ratings.

It is also vital for a starter to set standards that the broker's customer service should pass. In trading, brokers should work enough to earn the commission that they charge on the options that subscribers trade on buy. This is because some brokers are obscure and may not involve the options trader who is buying options in decisions that directly impact on his capital. One, therefore, faces a lot of anxiety if the broker is not responsive and transparent on the particular mechanics that influence trade.

Excellent broker services try to suit customer needs. They ask options traders subscribed to their platform what their preferred means of reaching is. Whether a live chat or phone call suits the customer or not. They also dedicate a desk for trading communications and queries and has the discipline to listen to customers and their issues with patience. They, in fact, have feedback on the quality of customer service that those who reach out get.

Software Trading Platforms

These are more complex than web-based ones. This is because they are run on the trader's computer, and the trader is required to understand what the software does and interpret it. Even when the brokerage can offer assistance, software-based platforms require the trader to have enough technical know how to read charts, graphs, and understand patterns that represent various components of options trading.

For beginners, a complex platform has to be avoided by all means. This is because one is bound to engage in aspects of trading that they do not have an understanding of. A trading platform simply has to be simple and clear. The interface should not be too busy as to scare away those traders who are not accustomed. This is the reason why operators usually separate the platforms that as designed for basic use, which is suitable for novices, and advanced trading for the seasoned ones.

Then a broker has to offer a tutorial that guides the user on how to navigate their platform. Everything has to be explained, even those that one would deem to be obvious. Screenshots can even be available in order to be categorical and emphatic. This ensures that a broker has offered all possible assists for the trader to benefit from the offers and products on the platform successfully.

Cost Implication

It is important for the trader to know that some brokers may have charges attached to some of the services, resources, and tools that they provide on their platform.

These have to be assessed in terms of their worth and whether the costs are necessary. Making some tolls premium may be an indicator of quality but not always. This is particularly the case when other platforms provide similar services toll-free.

Screening tools are particularly the ones that are bound to attract charges because they have abilities to analyze and assess market trends. They can do the thinking for the trader and help him in decision making. One has to read about the specifications of the tools and ascertain what they or cannot do. This is in order to know if they are customizable for the purpose of serving the needs and conveniences of traders.

Some charges can even be attached to the quotes update feed. Usually, the quotes can be accessed in real time for those who want to see them in real time. The quotes are important in influencing idea generation and sometimes can tip people of opportunities in the market. There is usually a delay for those who access the quotes updates for free.

It is also vital to understand platforms do not provide all the tools to everyone using their platform to trade. Some of the cutting-edge tools that can best serve the business interests of traders are premium. They have subscription charges or otherwise only appear on the accounts of traders who constantly sustain a certain threshold of account balance minimums. This is particularly the case for platforms that operate at the professional level. They require one to be active and remain active in trading since this serves the business interests of the brokerage through the commissions it earns on options contracts. In return, it offers the consultancy, expertise, and resource repository for one to realize value out of the options trades. This is why they attach a price on some of the tools.

Trading Platform

An electronic online trading platform is a computer software program that is used to place orders for day trading. The trading platform is different from the direct-access brokers themselves. However, I see often that traders confuse these two as one. The trading platform sends and places your order at the exchange so the direct-access brokers can clear the order for you. Usually direct-access brokers offer their own proprietary trading platform to their clients. The quality, charting capability, speed of the software, and many other features regarding the software, varies significantly, which also of course affects their pricing. Many brokers offer their platform for a monthly fee, but they may waive that fee if you make sufficient commissions for the broker. For example, Interactive Brokers offers a trading platform called Trader Workstation (TWS), but it also allows you to use the DAS Trader platform. Lightspeed Trading also offers its own platform called Lightspeed Trader. TD Ameritrade's own software is called thinkorswim. CenterPoint Securities uses DAS Trader as its platform.

The table below summarizes some of the well-known direct-access brokers for day trading. Please note that there are many more firms that are not listed below.

Broker	Trading Platform	PDT Restriction	Based In
Interactive Brokers	TWS or DAS Pro	Yes	USA
CenterPoint Securities	DAS Pro	Yes	USA
Lightspeed	Lightspeed Trader	Yes	USA
TD Ameritrade	thinkorswim	Yes	USA

Scottrade	ScottradeELITE	Yes	USA
E*TRADE	OptionsHouse	Yes	USA
Alliance Trader	DAS Pro	No	Jamaica
CMEG	DAS Pro	No	Trinidad and Tobago
SureTrader	DAS Pro	No	Bahamas

I also have a smaller account with CMEG at the time of writing. My broker, Interactive Brokers, offers their own platform called Trader Workstation or TWS, which I do not recommend for day trading. The DAS Trader platform is one of the four NASDAQ Platinum Partner order entry platforms that offer the highest level of efficient execution and market functionality for online traders. As mentioned earlier, DAS Trader is not a broker, it is only a trading platform, so I linked my IB trading account to it. When I enter my order in the platform, DAS will send my orders to NASDAQ data centers and Interactive Brokers, as my clearing firm, will fill my orders. I pay my trading commissions to IB and a monthly fee to DAS Trader for using their platform and providing me with a real time data feed and Level 2, which I will explain later in this book.

Fast trade execution is the key for day traders to be successful. You need to be able to move in and out of trades quickly. If your broker doesn't use a platform or software that has Hotkeys, you're not going to get in and out of trades fast enough. I can't tell you how many times I've been up a thousand dollars because all of a sudden the stock spiked. When the stock spikes, you want to be able to put money in your pocket and profit from it quickly. You definitely don't want to be fumbling with your orders. You need quick executions, which is why I highly recommend a good broker and also a fast order execution platform.

Candlesticks vs Bar Charts

The shadows are on top of the real body while the wicks are underneath the real body. The shadows are designed to display the low and high prices of the trading in a day.

If you look at a down candle, and you see that the top shadow is minute, then that means that the day's opening was close to the day's high worked.

If you notice that on an up day, you see a short shadow on top, then there was a high near the close. How the daily candlestick appears is dependent on the link that exists between the close, low, high, and open of the day.

Sometimes, the real bodies may come off as being white or black and short or long. Sometimes, the shadows may be short or long.

Similarly, candlestick charts and bar charts are known to offer similar details, but they do it in different methods. Candlestick chats tend to be a lot physical because of how it uses color on its price bars, as well as thicker real bodies. These are awesome when you want to tell the disparities between close and open.

Some traders love to see the hues and thickness of the candlestick charts, while others are in love with how neat the bar chart looks.

Basic Candlestick Patterns

When price movements occur whether up or down, these movements create the candlesticks.

Sometimes, these movements in price may come off as being random, but in other situations, they end up creating patterns that can be used by traders when they want to run the analysis.

There exist several candlestick patterns that you may see in a candlestick chart.

The normal patterns that you will see are bearish and bullish.

If you see Bullish patterns, you would know that the price has a higher probability of rising. If you see bearish patterns, it means that there is a high probability that the price would fall.

The truth is that you should not expect the pattern to function every time because candlestick patterns are meant to show the probability of price movements, and definitely no guarantees.

Bearish engulfing pattern

When the sellers in the market become higher than the buyers, you should notice a bearish engulfing pattern coming up. When this occurs, you will see a long red real body flaming up in a tiny green real body. This shows that the sellers are now in control, meaning that the price would most likely plummet.

Bullish engulfing pattern

If buyers are more than the sellers, you will notice a bullish engulfing pattern. This can be seen on the candle chart as a long green real body that engulfs a tiny red real body.

If the bulls at now in control, you will notice that the price would increase.

Bearish evening star

The evening star is seen as a topping pattern. You can see it in the pattern's last candle opening underneath the tiny real body of the prior day.

You may notice that the tiny real body is either of a greenish hue or red. The last candle ends up closing deeper in the candle's real body the day before yesterday.

If you see this pattern, it is important to know that buyers are stalling. Hence, sellers have more access to control. If care is not taken, there will be a lot of selling happening.

Bearish harami

You can tell the bearish harami if you notice a tiny red real body immersed into the real body of the prior day.

You shouldn't act on this pattern, but you can decide to analyze it. When you see the pattern, know that the buyers are feeling indecisive.

If this pattern shows and the price is still moving upward, then everything may turn out great. On the other hand, if you notice that a down candle is tailing this pattern, then there is a great chance of more slide.

Bullish harami

This is the exact opposite of the bearish harami. It can be said to be the upside down version.

In this pattern, you will notice a downtrend, as well as a tiny green real body showing in the big red real body of the prior day. If you see this, this means that the trend has paused. It may also mean that the upside is coming.

Bearish harami cross

You will see this a lot in an uptrend, showing that the Doji tails an up candle. The Doji is that part where the candlestick possesses an equal close and open.

In this pattern, the Doji is seen immersed in the previous session's real body. This has similar outcomes to a bearish harami.

Bullish harami cross

This happens in a downtrend, and here, the Doji follows the down candle. In this pattern, the Doji is immersed in the previous session's real body. This pattern bears similar outcomes to a bullish harami.

Bullish rising three

This pattern stands out in its black and white, though you will still see these hues in candlestick charts.

This type of patterns begins with a "long white day." On the other trading sessions of second, third, and fourth; the tiny real bodies reduce the price. This doesn't mean that they won't be in the price range of the long white day, which was seen on the first day of the pattern. On the last and fifth day, you will notice an extra long white day.

Bearish falling three

This pattern lets traders know that the price has been plummeting for three straight days, but it doesn't show a new low, meaning that a bull trader can get ready for another move up.

You may notice a minute difference in this pattern, which is the second day gapping up a bit, after the first day, it must have had a long up.

Apart from that, the other things are similar, though their appearance may seem a bit different. If you notice this difference, then it is a "bullish mat hold."

Usually, this begins having a strong down day. You will then see three tiny real bodies following it, making an upward movement, but this movement will be within the phase of the first large down day. This means that seller is now in control, meaning that the price may likely plummet.

Chapter 7 Common mistake with Day trading

Blind approach to day trading is bound to failure. Knowledge on day trading is not a one-day event; it's a lifetime process. Profit making on day trading is a difficult thing to do especially for starters because they lack discipline and consistency. Despite the difficulty involved in this venture, some practices can help raise or reduce your profit margins. It is essential for the newcomers in this industry to learn to do's, and the don'ts in day trading. Even though there is no guarantee these factors will assure you success in day trading, they will help you avoid trouble to some extent.

Unlike other businesses, making the right decisions in day trading has an almost immediate impact since a slight mistake here will cost you dearly. Whereas human emotion is not an essential factor in other business ventures, the success in day trading depends a lot on human emotion. To succeed here, you will be required to mold your thinking or even let go of your old practices.

Before getting into the trade market, it is essential to learn the risks involved in it. No amount of knowledge or research can make you guess the details of day trading. The best way of learning day trading tricks is by venturing into it. Whether you are in it or looking to venture into it, here are some of the Do's and the don'ts you should be aware of before taking on the trade.

Day trading tips and advice

Have A Trading Plan

A trading plan is an important factor for both the experienced and the newcomers in the trade market. Your plan should have all the details and aspects of your trading plan. Well, without a well-constructed plan, your venture will be more of gambling than trading. To achieve this effectively, seek knowledge of how to create a good trading plan from the experienced stock traders.

Be A Realist

Always be realistic about the kind of profits you expect from the trade market. Do not let greed make you lose your decent gains. Stock markets are tricky and competitive; it is, therefore, better for you to settle for small profits rather than losing out everything. If you lose a chance, do not beat yourself up; instead, wait for the next opportunity to present itself. A slight gain or profit boosts your confidence in the stock market.

A Strict Routine Is Important

Trading is a lonely endeavor without a boss to tell you what to do or what not to do. Therefore, a strict routine will help put you overcome the challenge of self-discipline. If it is hard for you to follow a strict trading schedule, your career as an independent trader may be far from success. Therefore, self-discipline is an essential character that anyone looking to succeed in the day trade needs to have.

Never Stop Learning

Exhausting knowledge is something no human being can do or has ever done. Even though there are plenty of quick learning systems that have been put out there for new coming traders, learn the art of day trade from scratch. It will give you a better chance to succeed. It is essential that you learn the trade using your interpretation as opposed to learning it from anyone else. Even though different trading strategies that have worked for others can work for you, market conditions differ. By doing so, you will gain more confidence in your trading abilities.

Always Seek Professional Advice

It is essential to follow a given coaching program to succeed in day trading. By doing so, time for exploration will be minimized. Even though experimentation is a good practice in day trading, seek knowledge from the experienced traders. Study shows that 90% of traders who lose money during their entry to the trade market do not end their careers well.

Set A Limit On Losses

Day trading is a game where profits and losses are two of the most critical factors. You cannot stay in a business where you are consistently losing your money. Therefore, it is essential for you to set your loss limit. Once you hit your limit, decide whether you want to continue trading or exit the market.

Apply Macro And Micro Idea Generation

A good marketer is quick in identifying opportunities in the market. Day trading is full of competition; therefore, it is important always to beat the biases. Know the factors to look at when identifying a good opportunity. Macro and micro factors have direct effects on the trading market. Therefore, it is essential to correlate events, drivers and indicators affecting day trade market.

Concentrate On Fundamental Analysis

As a stock trader, it is vital that you learn and understand your company well. Factors such as financial information concerning your company should be in your fingertips. Through that, you will ascertain the capability and the health situation of your company. An excellent investment opportunity is that which has the stock price trading below the company's intrinsic value. The fundamental reason why most traders do not rely on fundamental analysis is that most traders spend a few days in the market.

Do The Technical Analysis

This is looking at the current stock price and currency. Analyze these factors to understand the direction the stock marketing may be taking. Also, look at the historical performance and the current stock price. These tools will help you in determining the market direction.

Do Action

Once you understand the market well, and you feel confident about your next move, do not hesitate to make a move. Did you know that timing can make or break your chances of making it in the stock market? Regardless of the direction of the market, it is essential for you to set your targets to take your profits as you place your limits.

Always Control Your Emotions

The pace and events of day trading can be so tiring. Its experience can be intense and often draining mentally. A beginner will find this difficult, but once you learn to control your emotions, you will be a successful trader. The two most fundamental traits that are likely to take control of you are greed and fear. If you are not keen, the two attributes will take control of you, and you are likely to fail. Do not exit too quickly when everything is going your way because of fear. However, do not also let it run too long, in case of a constant downfall, take out your profits before it all dries up.

Do Have A Limit

To maximize your profits, use the golden rule where you apply 'stop losses' and 'soft limits' policy. This means that your previous lowest point or highest point placed close to stop losses. In a case where the market is moving to a position you anticipated, then it's your perfect chance to let your position move. The most important thing here is that you maximize your gains. The number of commodities and stocks should be under control. Every stock is unique in its way. Therefore, with time, you will learn the tricks, and your judgment will improve with experience.

Mistakes Are Allowed

The moment you get into the stock market, failures and setbacks is the norm of business. A perception that only the newcomers are bound to make mistakes is wrong; even the most experienced stock traders make mistakes. A common mistake made by most day traders is the time of entry or exit in the market. Through these mistakes, you will be able to predict and execute better. As discussed above, seeking knowledge from the experienced traders will help minimize your mistakes in the market. Once you get into the market, you will realize that what you experience is different from what you learned from books. The best teacher in any stock market, therefore, is an experience.

Take Note At Every Mistake As You Improve

Losing a trade is not the end of the world in the stock market. Instead, use it a learning process. Compare what you expected in the market to what you received. Identifying the mistakes you committed and the underlying factors that might have contributed to your failure.

How to control your emotion after recording a loss

Do Not Take Huge Risks

Avoid greed at all cost when it comes to day trading. Before taking any risk, look at the possibility of losing the money. If you cannot cope with the possibility of losing, then it is not worth investing your money. Always keep in mind that even with the best strategies, the chances of winning investment in a stock market is 50/50. Also, take time to learn the exact ratios that apply in the stock market since they fluctuate from time to time.

Don't Invest With The Intention Of Revenge

As a human being, you are likely to respond to an inevitable failure with a vengeance. Never approach day trade with such plan since you are likely to fail terribly. In case of a failure, sit back and study to know the cause of your failures. Take time to strategize your next move. I can assure you that getting into the market an intention of revenge will cause you more harm than good.

Do Not Trade Too Many Times

It is advisable for you to trade once in a while. Only put on an investment when an excellent opportunity presents itself. Proper analysis is important before putting your money on any stock market. However, you can spend as much time as you can analyze the market situation instead of doing the actual trading. Quit spending too much time trading since it is a recipe for disaster.

Do Not Scalp If You Are New In The Market

Scalping is merely taking a short cut by taking on trades that last only for a few seconds. Even though scalping is a good way of making good money, it is precarious. You need a certain level of skill and experience to understand and predict a sudden shift in market movements. In every trade you take, you are required to pay spread fee notwithstanding the direction taken by any trade. Therefore, experience and knowledge are essential since you have got to achieve pips above the spread cost.

It is important to take notes as you try different strategies. Stock marketplace, experience, and knowledge are the two most important factors.

Do Not Trust Unreliable Sources Of Information

Often you receive emails, text messages or advertisement claiming a good profit on any stocks. Not that you shut down such sources, ensure the information they give are authentic and reliable. As a good trader, be careful not to fall into the hands of brokers who are hungry for commotions. These people can easily land you into bad trade hence losses.

Keep Away From Penny Stocks

As a starter in day trading, penny stocks should be the last thing you should do. Experienced traders will tell you that you should not engage in a trade that is difficult to exit. Also, penny stocks are highly illiquid; hence your chances of hitting huge profits are low.

Do Not Refuse To Take Out Your Profits

It natural for any human being to want more or never get satisfied with whatever they have since everyone is in business to make an extra coin. Moreover, a mistake comes in when you want to make quick money. As a result, every trader wants to make unimaginable profits with their first trade. However, in the stock market what looks like a huge gain could end up to be a huge loss. Well, expecting a huge gain from your trade is not bad. However, it is essential to be realistic about the kind of profits you expect from your investment.

Winning vs Losing in Day trading

Most people follow the world of online trading closely. Interestingly, some of these people never invest in trading. Well, it is not a bad thing to follow and understand how trading could impact your financial goals. However, you also need to realize that there are benefits of trying out the idea of trading. Win or lose, there is something important which you will learn from the activity. So, if you have never traded before, you shouldn't be afraid to try. After all, there is no harm in trying. Keep in mind that there are various brokers who will help you initiate your trading activity without having to use your funds. This is made possible by using free demo accounts.

Knowing that there is something in store for you whether you win or lose in day trading should motivate you in taking the right steps to become a trader. Traders who have been in business for some time will argue that there is a rewarding feeling in learning something from an exciting activity like day trading. Some life lessons which you will learn in the process of trading are briefly discussed in the following lines.

Enhanced Decision Making
Online trading requires one to develop a sound decision-making process as this will lead to the best results. By constantly finding a way to improve the decision-making process, a trader also increases their chances of earning

good returns. The notion of doing this will ultimately have a positive impact on one's life. When a trader seeks to improve how well they make their decisions, they also end up affecting their day to day decisions. This means that the quality of life of any trader would considerably be improved.

Self-Awareness

With online trading, there is a guarantee that you will develop a sense of self-awareness you might have never had before. Succeeding in online trading demands that a trader should always keep their emotions in check. Trading with emotions will often cloud your judgment. For example, you might stay too long on a trade without selling out. Also, you could be tempted to enter a trade just because you have nothing to do. At the end of the day, you will incur losses because your decision-making process is clouded.

In real life situations, there are many times when we are blinded from perceiving life with objectivity. Most of the decisions we end up making affect our personal lives. By choosing to learn how to succeed in day trading, you will also learn how to make sound decisions in life without allowing your emotions to come in the way. The best part is that you will also learn how to appreciate things the way they are. Simply stated, this is the kind of personality that day trading requires any trader.

Entrepreneurship Skills

Interestingly, the skills you obtain while day trading could be applied in other businesses that you might be running. There is no business that doesn't have risks. To succeed in business, you need to know the existence of risks which could negatively affect your business. Similarly, you need to learn how to mitigate such risks using feasible solutions. When you choose to engage in online trading, you get all these lessons for free. The strategies you employ to lower your risks can be used in ensuring that your businesses always thrive. So, as earlier mentioned, whether you succeed or fail in day trading, there is something good you will be taking home.

Uncertainty Is Your Closest Friend

Nothing is guaranteed when engaging in online trading. Markets can move in any direction. Therefore, you could either make profits or losses depending on how you predicted the markets to perform. In real life situations, there is nothing we are always certain about. Whether you are opening a new business or taking on a new venture you have never tried before, it is all about uncertainty. Trading in securities over the internet will help you a mentality where you accept that uncertainty is your closest friend.

Taking Risks and Reducing Risk

Most people are afraid to try online trading because of its associated risks. In fact, a common myth you will hear from traders who have failed is that day trading is too risky and unprofitable. This is not the case. You will only lose on day trading when you fail to implement the best strategies. For instance, you need to have a risk mitigation strategy as well as an overall trading strategy. Knowing how to stomach huge risks with the anticipation of making profits is not easy. This is an art. Very few people are willing to take risks in their lives. This is the number one reason why most entrepreneurs fail. Choosing not to take a risk can prove to be costly. This is because one might end up losing out in an opportunity that would have transformed their lives. So, day trading will teach you a lot about taking risks and reducing risks.

Importance of Diversification

The phrase "you should not put all your eggs in one basket" applies to numerous life situations. Whether in business or your career, it is always important to diversify. Diversifying your activities prevents you from making huge losses. In business, diversifying guarantees that you make profits even when one of your businesses is not working out. For instance, if you are offering two products to the market, through diversification, you can be sure that one of the products will perform well. Day trading will teach you that it is important to diversify as it helps you spread your risks. Therefore, it is a valuable lesson for most people.

Looking Beyond Financial Gains

There are numerous times that you must have been told to have passion in whatever you do. Well, this is true for most businesses. The only way that you will truly succeed in business in your career is by falling in love with what you do. Day trading will be a good training school. It will help you understand that it is more than just the money you are after. When trading using smaller accounts, your focus will be on getting experience and learning how to trade. Ideally, your aim is learning something new from the trading activity. Therefore, there is a rewarding feeling in knowing that you are a better trader today than yesterday. With this mentality, you will live to appreciate the idea of gaining experience from any activity you engage in. Hence, if you will be opening up a new store around the corner and it fails to succeed, you will be happy you tried and failed than failing to try completely.

I hope you see how day trading could impact your life in many ways. If you have the right mentality when you are entering any trading market, you will enjoy the activity over the long haul. Don't believe the hype that is out in the streets. Have confidence that your plan works in spite of the few losses here and there. As always, you should motivate yourself with the notion that even the most experienced of traders incur huge losses. So, before you think that day trading will not help you in any way, think twice.

Chapter 8 Choosing Your Day Trading Securities

If you want to execute a profitable day trade, it all begins and ends with choosing the "right" securities for day trading. Many newbie day traders give up easily because of mostly losing trades, not knowing that the primary reason for their losing trades is the inability to choose their securities well. Don't make the same mistake.

If you choose securities whose prices are as animated as a person on valium or whose trading volume is as high as that of a small private corporation operating in the Himalayan mountains, forget about profitable day trading. When it comes to day trading, it behooves you to learn two of the most powerful statements among traders, which are:

"Volatility isn't your enemy but your friend. Your best friend."

and

"You're only as good as the securities you trade."

Think of it this way, the only way you can make profitable day trades is when prices of securities go up or down during the day, depending on whether you're long or short. If prices are relatively flat, how can you hit your profit-taking price target?

Remember securities in play or SIP? Well, there are multiple ways to identify and select them. Some traders go for individual securities themselves, e.g., shares of stock of a particular company, a particular currency pair, or a particular cryptocurrency. Some trade a collection or package of securities, e.g., exchange-traded funds (ETFs). Some prefer to trade markets as a whole through securities like index futures contracts.

Remember, SIPs offer very good risk-reward ratio opportunities. And the good news is you can regularly monitor a SIP that may possibly go above or beyond its current market price because SIPs typically move frequently and with high levels of predictability.

There are new SIPs daily, which can give you opportunities to trade your funds optimally by providing very good risk-reward ratios during the day.

Securities in Play

What are stocks in play, again? They're securities that can be one or all of the following:

Securities that have significant new developments or news;

Securities whose prices are above or below the previous day's by at least 2% prior to market opening for the day;

Securities whose prices have moved significantly during the trading day; and

Securities with uncommon activities prior to market opening.

Keep in mind that when talking about securities with high trading volumes, we're talking about relative trading volume and not absolute trading volumes. What's the difference?

Let's compare two stocks, A and B. Stock A's average trading volume is 500,000 shares, while Stock B's average trading volume is 20 million shares. Stock B has a very high absolute trading volume compared to Stock A's daily average of only 500,000, which is considered low compared to Stock B's.

If Stock A's trading volume for the last 3 days between 900,000 to 1 million shares, while Stock B's trading volume for the same period was 22 million shares, Stock A has a higher relative trading volume for that period of time. Why?

Stock A's trading volume for the last three days is higher than its average by at least 400,000 shares, which is 80% of its average daily trading volume of 500,000 shares. Stock B's trading volume for the same period on the other hand, is higher than its daily average trading volume of 20 million shares by 2 million shares, which is only 10% of its average daily volume.

Because Stock A's trading volume for the last three days is up by at least 80% from its long-term daily average compared to only 10% for Stock B, Stock A has a very high relative trading volume compared to Stock B.

One of the reasons for choosing securities with high relative trading volume as compared to absolute trading volume is because more likely than not, low relative trading volume securities are being dominated by large trading institutions that use HFT computer programs, which retail day traders like us need to avoid.

When looking for high relative trading volume securities, remember that they need to be securities that trade independently from the entire market or their industry/sector. To get a general idea of how a particular security's market or sector's moving, just check out their major indexes. In the case of stocks, it's the Dow Jones Industrial Average or the S&P 500 index. When they're down, chances are that most stocks are down as well. When they're going up, chances are high that most stocks are going up as well.

Because high relative volume securities prices move independently from their respective markets, they're considered as securities in play or SIPs. There are only a few SIPs in the market every day, which are also referred to as "alpha" securities because they're on top of the list and nobody rules over them. Stick to such securities that have fundamental reasons or triggers for price movements for your day trading activities.

One of the things that set securities in motion or in play is freshly released and important news about or that can impact a particular security. And by freshly released, I mean the day before or during the trading day itself.

If it's stocks, it could be just-released corporate earnings or a newly-signed joint venture agreement with a major investor. It could also be news on the passage of a law that could restrict the business activities of that particular company. Such news can substantially impact investors' sentiment about that stock, which could make it move significantly in either direction.

Market Capitalization and Float

Float refers to the number of units of a particular security that's currently circulating or "floating" in the market. It could be the number of shares of stock of companies like Apple that are available in the market or the number of tokens of Bitcoin circulating on cryptocurrency exchanges.

Market capitalization refers to how much all of those shares or units in the market are worth. If there are 1 million shares of Stock A in circulating in the market today and its current market price is $5.00 per share, then Stock A's current market capitalization is $5 million, which will change accordingly as its stock prices goes up and down.

For optimal day trading purposes, low float and low market capitalization stocks are the way to go. Why?

Remember how volatility is a trader's best friend because it provides the profit opportunities that traders are looking for? Securities that have a bazillion units or shares floating in the market or have huge market capitalization (also called mega cap securities) are not likely to provide the volatility needed for profitable day trading. Why?

It would take a lot of units or shares and money to affect the prices significantly. The prices of securities that have low float and market capitalization (also called micro-cap securities) can be much more easily influenced because they neither need a lot of trading volume nor a lot of money to move.

And when looking for profitable day trading opportunities, you'll want to stick with securities that are volatile and not those that are steady.

For consistency purposes of discussions moving forward, I'll use stocks as financial securities that we'll day trade. This is because stocks are the most popular and easiest to understand financial security for day trading purposes.

Now that we've clarified that, let's take a look at three float categories of stocks that can be day traded:

Low float stocks that are less than $10 per share;

Medium float stocks that are between $10 to $100 per share; and

Mega cap stocks like Yahoo, Intel, Facebook, and Google, among others.

Stocks that have low float and are trading at less than $10 per share are very volatile. Just how volatile can they be? Their prices can swing by as much as 100% in a single trading day!

Because of their very high volatility, they provide the biggest potential for day trading profits. However, you must be very careful trading these stocks because they can swing the other way and much of your trading money in one fell swoop if you don't monitor them closely and act swiftly.

Because of their low float and prices, stocks under this category are very vulnerable to price manipulation by traders with a lot of trading ammo. As such, they can be very challenging for a newbie or inexperienced day traders. Because of the wild price swings, the chances of burning most of one's trading capital in a single day are high for newbie traders. Usually, only those with a whole lot of day trading experience and tools day trade stocks under this category.

Another thing to keep in mind with low float stocks below $10 per share is that they're not ideal for short-selling. Why?

One reason is that brokers are often reluctant to lend volatile stocks because of the high probability that prices spike rapidly and prevent those that borrow them from paying them back.

Another reason why such stocks aren't ideal is that their prices can swing wildly within a short period of time that it can wipe out a newbie day trader's account. If you want to minimize your day trading risks, especially as a newbie, it's best to leave this category of stocks to the experienced and sophisticated day traders for the meantime.

The second category of day trading stocks are medium float ones whose market prices hover between $10 to $100. By medium float, I mean around 10 to 500 million shares are circulating in the market. Most of the strategies we'll cover later on work well with stocks under this category. They provide just enough volatility to earn substantial money but not too volatile that newbie day traders are at high risk for losing most of their money in just one day.

The third category of stocks, the mega capitalized ones, have over half-a-billion shares floating in the market, which gives them a very huge market capitalization. So huge that only big, institutional traders can significantly impact their market prices.

This category should be off limits for retail day traders like you and I, unless there's a really good fundamental catalyst for moving their prices significantly within the day. But even then, it's best to avoid them as much as possible, considering that large institutional and HFT-powered traders dominate this category.

How to Find Stocks (Securities) in Play

You can do this using two tactics: through a watchlist just before markets open in the morning and real-time scanning of the market during the trading day. You'll need a good market scanning program for this to make both processes fast, efficient, and accurate.

For the morning, pre-market open scan, program your trading app or software to scan the market for stocks that meet the following conditions:

Stocks that already had a minimum of 50,000 shares change hands during the pre-market opening;

Stocks whose average daily price range is at least $0.50 per share, i.e., the difference between their highest and lowest prices for the day;

Stocks whose prices are down or up by at least 2% during the pre-market opening from the previous day's closing prices;

Stocks whose short interest, i.e., uncovered short-sold shares, of at most 30% of total short-sold shares;

Stocks with an average daily trading volume of at least 500,000 shares; and/or

Stocks with significant fundamental catalysts for their stock price movements.

The reason for setting the above as criterions for choosing stocks in play or SIPs is because when fundamental catalysts or triggers are present for certain shares, pre-market activity for such stocks will be much higher than usual (e.g., more than 50,000 shares traded during pre-market) and will most likely have registered a price gap of at least 2% in either direction.

With stocks that have high relative trading volume, liquidity risk is low, which means you can quickly take and close your day trading positions. For this, average trading volumes of at least 500,000 fit the bill.

Stocks with a minimum daily price range of at least $0.50 can provide necessary volatility for meaningful day trading profits. Remember, volatility is your day trading best friend together with high liquidity.

Sometimes, your trading program's won't find stocks that match these criterions. What should you do then?

It's time to shift to Plan B, which is scanning the market during actual trading hours. In particular, you'll want to look for SIPs for top reversal, bottom reversal, and momentum trades. The reason for scanning for these stocks during trading hours is because they can be hard to find during the pre-market.

Chapter 9 Money Management

The truth is that a lot of traders, especially novices, started with a lot in their trading accounts and at the end of the day, they had little or nothing to boast about. Many of them lost their funds because of thoughtless actions or not following a well-crafted strategy. To manage your money well, there are some things that you have to do.

Choose The Right Lot Size Based On Your Capital

When you start at forex training or financial market trading, you will tend to learn about trading lots. What we mean by a lot is the tiniest trade size available that can be placed when you decide to trade currency pairs on the foreign exchange market.

Usually, brokers tend to talk about lots using increments of a thousand or a micro lot. You have to understand that the lot size determines directly, as well as shows that risk among that you are willing to take.

Using a risk management calculator or a top like that can help you know what the right lot size is, based on what your trading account assets are currently. This can be used either when you are trading live or you are merely practicing. It allows you to know what amount that can be risked.

The trading lot size affects how the market movements can affect the accounts. Let's use an example.

When a 100-pip move occurs, it won't have so much effect on a small trade like similar 100-pip move on a trade size that is quite massive.

As a trader, you will see several lot sizes.

We will explain the lots as follow:

Trading With Micro Lots

The tiniest tradable lots that can be used are called mini lots. A micro lot has a thousand units of the currency that is in your account. If you have funded your account with USD, a micro-lot of that has a value of a thousand dollars, as the base currency.

If you have decided to trade a dollar-based pair, a pip means ten cents.

As a beginner, it is favorable to use micro lots as it reduces your risk, while you practice trading.

Mini lots have ten thousand units of the currency that you use to fund your account. If you are making use of an account that has dollars as its base currency, then every pip in the trade would be valued at around $1.00.

As a beginner that wants to begin with mini lots, it is advisable that you are adequately capitalized.

A dollar per pip may seem quite tiny, but the market sometimes even gets to a hundred pips daily. Sometimes, this may happen in one hour.

If the forex market isn't moving in your direction, this means that you have made a loss of a hundred dollars.

It is you that will choose your ultimate risk tolerance. Before you can trade a mini account, it is advisable that you don't mind using at least two thousand dollars.

Using Standard Lots

A standard lot has a hundred thousand units of the base currency in a trading account. If you have a base currency of dollars, this is a hundred thousand dollar lots. The normal pip size for a standard lot is ten dollars for every pip.

When the trade is against you by ten pip, this is a loss of hundred dollars. This type of lot is used by institutional-sized accounts.

What this translates to is that you should possess at least $25,000 to be able to carry out trades using standard lots.

A lot of forex traders tend to make use of either micro lots or mini lots.

To a novice, this may not seem glamorous, but when you keep the lot size proportional to the size of your account, your trading capital will be preserved, and you can easily trade with it for a long while.

Let's use an illustration;

Using a small trade size compared to what you have in your account can be likened to strolling on a sturdy bridge that has shelter to prevent any issue from worrying you. It doesn't matter if heavy rain occurs; you will be sheltered.

If you place a big trade size when compared to the account funds, it can be likened to walking on a narrow bridge. In this case, the bridge is fragile and narrow, meaning that you can fall at any time. A tiny movement in the market could toss you away, and lead you to a spot that you can't return from.

Below are some things you should consider before you begin.

Do not let your gain become a loss

One thing that has been noticed is that a lot of forex traders tend to turn their profit into a loss. The forex market worldwide does at least $5 trillion daily. This has made it the most significant financial market globally.

The fact that Forex is lucrative has made it popular amongst a lot of traders from novices to experts in the field.

Since it is quite easy to get involved in forex because of the little costs, round-the-clock sessions, and so on, it is also straightforward to lose your capital as you trade forex.

To ensure that your gain doesn't turn to a loss as a forex trader, you should try and avoid some mistakes.

Learn, Learn and Learn

The fact that it is quite easy to get involved in forex has led a lot of people to get involved without bothering to learn. To succeed in forex or any financial market for that matter, you need to learn. You should learn from live trading, experience, as well as reading up on forex literature. Don't forget the news. You spiel find out about economic and geopolitical factors that have effects on the preferred currencies of a trader.

The world of forex is ever changing meaning that you must keep yourself abreast with these changes in the regulations, market conditions, as well as global events.

While you undergo the research process, you should also consider creating a trading plan.

This plan should involve a method where you can screen and analyze investments, in a bid to determine how much risk should be expected when creating investment goals.

Use only a reputable broker

The truth is that the forex world isn't so regulated, unlike others, meaning that you may end up carrying out business with unscrupulous brokers. It is advisable that you only open an account with a National Futures Association (NFA) member if you want your deposits to be safe, and you are interested in the integrity of that broker. Use only brokers that are listed as futures commission merchant with the regulatory body of your country. If the broker isn't registered, avoid them.

It is also advisable that you study the account offerings of the brokers like commissions, leverage amounts, spreads, account withdrawal and funding policies and so on. You can find these out by talking to a customer service representative.

Utilize a practice account

Almost every trading platform out there has a practice account. This is also called a demo account or a simulated account.

The account permits traders to carry out hypothetical trades that do not need a funded account. Using a perceive account allows the trader to get used to order-entry techniques quickly.

Using a practice account allows the trader to learn, thereby avoiding a lot of mistakes in their trading account.

We had seen cases of when a novice trader erroneously adds to a losing position, when he intended to close the trade.

Several errors in the order entry could worsen to a big losing trade. Losing funds is not the only issue; you have to also battle with a stressful and annoying situation.

There is nothing wrong if you decide to try out order entries before you start to place the real money on live trading.

Keep Your Charts clean

When a forex trader creates an account, he or she may be tempted to use every tech assessment tool available in the trading platform.

A lot of these indicators are high in the foreign exchange market, but it is advisable that you reduce the hunger of analysis methods that you use to be efficient.

Making use of several similar kinds of indicators like three oscillators or as three volatility indicators may come off as being unnecessary. Sometimes, you may even get opposite signals. You should try and avoid this.

If you aren't using an analysis technique well, you should consider taking it out of your chart. It is also essential that you look at the total appearance of the workspace.

The hues, kinds and fonts of price hard such as candle bar, line, range bar, and so on that you use should craft out an easy-to-read-and-interpret chart, permitting you to respond to the ever-changing conditions in the market quickly.

Stop Loss Order Is Not Just For Preventing Losses

Stop loss orders are used a lot in preventing losses, but it does more than that. It can also be used in locking profits. If used for this, it is sometimes called a "trailing stop."

At this point, the stop-loss order is being set at a per cent height that is beneath what the current market price is, and different from the price that it was bought at.

The stop loss's price fluctuates the same way the price of the stock adjusts.

What this means is that if the price of a stock increases, you may have to battle with an unrealized gain. This means that you won't have the money with you until after the sales.

Making use of trailing stop permits you to allow your run, and still guarantee you an amount of realized capital gain.

It is important that you note that the stop-loss order will always be a market order, meaning that it would lie low, until the trigger price has been reached. This means that the price your stock may sell for may end up being a bit different from what you specified as your trigger price.

Benefits of stop loss order

One thing that we all love about stop loss is the fact that we don't have to pay a dime to implement it. The normal commission is only charged when you have reached stop-loss price and your stock has been sold. What you should see it as is a free insurance policy.

Using a stop loss ensured that decisions are made based on facts, taking out any form of emotional influence.

Many people end up crushing on their stocks, feeling that if they allowed the stock to stay on, it would surely succeed, even when the facts are saying another story. This leads to delay and procrastination on the part of the trader, and before you know it, he is raking in unimaginable losses.

It doesn't matter what kind of trader you see yourself as; there must be a reason you have decided to own a stock.

The criteria listed by a value investor is usually different from the one listed by a growth investor and an active trader.

You have to create a good strategy and stick to it. What we want you to do is to trust in your strategy and follow through with it. With stop loss orders, it is easy to remain on track, and wipe off the emotional judgement.

One thing that you should also note is that using stop loss orders does not necessarily mean that you will end up earning in the financial market.

To earn, you have to make rational judgements in real time. If you are unable to do this, you will end up losing the same money you would have lost without the use of stop loss, but it would be at a slower rate.

The stop loss order is one tool that is easy to use, but a lot of investors do not utilize it. Every investing style can easily benefit from this tool. See it as a type of insurance policy, and you will be grateful.

Putting your Stop at Pockets of Liquidity

Some price structures tend to be continuously raided for liquidity before the financial market tries to reverse.

Try to avoid putting your stop loss order either directly underneath or above:

Important swing lows and highs,

Clean equal lows and highs.

Avoiding this is done because there may be the probability that the market may end up trading via them before a reversal occurs.

Get out a price chart of that market that you are in, and tick those clean equal lows and highs, range lows and highs and key swing spots.

In a lot of scenarios, you will end up seeing that the price tends to trade via these structures before they move the other way.

Those traders that have their stops below or above the structures directly are usually thrown out of whatever portions that they were in. The market then ends up moving in the predicted direction without their existence.

How to shield yourself from getting hunted.

The truth is that doing this isn't so easy, and that's why it is quite useful in any market. This occurs especially when you make use of self-executing orders, as well as when you are not always at the screen looking a the price when it gets to those important aspects.

To prove yourself, don't out your stop loss order in undeniable places.

Places like range boundaries, swing points, as well as equal wicks are easily noticed, and that is the reason they are usually targeted when runs for liquidity occur.

Avoid the temptation to utilize them as your reference point when you have decided to leave the orders in that financial market.

If you like yourself, it is advisable that you create some space between any of the structures listed about, as well as your stop loss order.

This allows the price to wick via the low or high, without the thought of you being knocked out.

Always Keeping To One Stop Level

We earlier mentioned that the reason you have a stop is to shield your account from so much loss when your trade idea becomes wrong.

Sometimes, you have to move your stop. You are wondering if I am playing with you. No. We advised against this because moving it to a break-even means that you aren't relying on technicals to take what the market is offering you.

When you decide to move your stop loss order and when the market shows that it is moving in the predicted direction, you are doing so based on the technicals at hand. Only move your stop when the technicals tell you to do so.

We should state the difference clearly. The first one is merely an emotional decision in order for you to get the feeling of safety.

On the other hand, the second one is done based on what the technicals sow because you want to retain a great R:R when the price goes to the target.

Chapter 10 Data Analysis

The stock analysis involves fundamental analysis and technical analysis, all relating to searching for information about a given stock. The traditional stock analysis involves learning the history of stock trading. When doing fundamental analysis, it will entail learning about the business and its environment. The essential tools when doing fundamental analysis include the overall financial position documents as well as Securities and Exchange Commission filings. Most people avoid fundamental analysis on the notion that it is tiresome and time-consuming. However, you can greatly benefit from the information it provides. In doing technical analysis, it will require you to know the recognizable patterns, current price trend, and historical price movement of stocks. When analyzing, you should look at the stock with the biggest percentage gains from the previous day. It should be followed by looking at chart breakouts.

Interesting and most suitable stocks to choose are earning winners and contract winners. The advantage of identifying which stocks fall in the noted classifications is that one does not need to comprehend complex financial statements. For instance, you can search for stock spike, which is simple to identify. When looking for contract winners, you can search for the press release of small companies that are signing deals with big companies. If the deal is legit, then there will be a spike in its stock price. Also, trading volumes are good indicators of a possibly good stock. As a trader, you should stay away from a company whose stock has fallen by a significant percentage, such as 50 percent in a day.

At this point, you have equipped yourself with important information about potential stocks that you can trade. To avoid spreading yourself too thin, it would be good to limit yourself to five to ten stocks. It should begin with the strong to the weak market sectors. Also, you have to ensure that each of the stocks included in the watchlist has potential trade triggers, ensuring that you have planned the trade triggers ahead of time. This is why you considered the stock in your watchlist. Prior planning will entail having the legwork done in the pre-market to ensure that you will be ready when a given trigger forms. We noted that a trigger is that which determines whether you will buy or sell a given stock. Experts in the market describe a suitable stock as "shovel ready." The implication in this is that you can immediately take a given action on a stock when an indicator triggers.

Also, we noted that a watchlist entails those stocks that fit your trading strategies. You should actualize this by ensuring that you are honest with your trading style. Take, for instance, an intraday scalper. For such a person, the most suitable stocks will be those that follow through and have good momentum and volatility. Also, those stocks that are gapping on a catalyst event or on the news are best suited for such traders. How will you carry out good scalping? The best way to do this will be by implementing shorter time frame charts. A swing trader will focus on different things. These include targeting less volatile and slow moving stocks because they allow for longer holding periods.

Other important considerations are liquidity and volume. While you may wonder why you should bother with these aspects, it is important to note that volume to a certain degree ensures liquidity, while liquidity supersedes price. A good or tradable stock is that which meets both conditions, as they prevent you from being disadvantaged. You should avoid a stock that has no volume. In doing so, you are proving to be selective to the best opportunities. In doing this, you will have to ensure that you do not waste time on mundane prospects.

The other trick is to set alerts for intraday and swing trades. It is not as complex as it sounds, because most charting programs and trading platforms allow the users to set alerts. It has proven to be a reliable technology because constant monitoring of stocks could be tiresome. You can set alerts depending on indicator triggers or price. However, ensure that you separate swing trade alerts from day trading alerts. The essence of alerts is that they allow you to maximize your focus when needed.

When you have implemented the noted guidelines and familiarize yourself with trading, you will realize that you are well versed with information. With time, you will see that your watchlist is growing large. At this point, having multiple and diverse watchlists categorized differently is beneficial. The categories may include long-term investment stocks, sector plays, swing plays, and short-term stocks.

How do you approach Fundamental Analysis?

We are now ready to explore fundamental analysis more. The reason we talked about the economic release is that one of the main sources of data for fundamental analysis is the information provided by the release. But additionally, fundamental analysis also includes political data as sometimes politics can influence the economic regulations and advancements of a country. In fact, the politics of the country can indicate the confidence various factions have with the government of the country and this, in turn, can reveal the status of factors such as foreign investments.

Fundamental analysis also includes the review of macroeconomic indicators and the stock market as well.

When working with fundamental analysis, the existing inflation rate, foreign currency, and monetary mass all come into play. For this reason, governments have increased the frequency of the releases so that traders are able to compare them easily with previous reports. This makes it easier to generate forecasts about the direction the currency is taking and how it could evolve in the near future.

Traders typically start with the primary analysis of data and several factors are important for this analysis:

• Economic growth: Traders usually discover this by using the quarterly published figure of the country's GDP. When traders notice that the GDP of a country is rising, then that typically signifies a shift in the capital. This shift occurs because there has been a rise in the savings and consumption in the country. Traders value the consumption increase and make their trades accordingly, having positive sentiments about the currency. However, an excess of growth is not a good indicator. This is because there are chances that the country could eventually deal with inflation tensions and force the Central Banks to change their interest rates.

• Inflation: Typically, when currencies have high-interest rates they are considered favorable because of the fact that they can contain inflation rates and of course, the chance to attain high profits. Which is why, when looking at inflation, traders will also look at the Central Bank's changes.

• Unemployment: The rate of unemployment is sometimes difficult to measure accurately, but it is nonetheless a very important component and indicator for traders. The main reason for this is that it determines the consumption and income levels for families. If the unemployment rates rise, then the currency of the country falls so hard that it might just punch a hole through the financial basement. When the unemployment rates drop, it helps elevate the currency's value.

• Trade Balance: A currency quote can attain an equilibrium, which happens when there is stability in the balance of payments. If the country has a trade deficit, then it suffers due to a drop in the currency reserves, which eventually causes a drop in the value of the currency as well.

• Stock market: Inflation, growth, and even unemployment are just some of the factors that are involved in finding out the value of the currency. Every single day, the evolution of a currency has a big impact on the assets markets, in particular, stocks. When investors have positive sentiments about a country, then they increase investments into that country, which in turn propels the stocks and assets to new heights. With the arrival of different currencies into the market, the value of the currency of the home country will become strong.

How Do You Use Fundamental Analysis?

The fundamental analysis is a bit different compared to what to some of the other strategies that we find in this guidebook. While most of the other strategies ask you to take a look at the graphs around a stock and then determine when you want to invest and when you want to get out of the market, the fundamental analysis is going to look more at the company that is behind the stock, and how that company is doing.

The fundamental analysis is often going to look at a variety of factors behind the stock and factors that may not influence the price right now but could in the future. It looks to see who is running the business, what changes they are planning to make in the future if there is any change in the management, the debt to profit ratio of the company and more. It basically looks to see how financially secure the company is, something that isn't necessarily going to show up in the stock charts you look at.

They aren't really that interested in what the price will do past that time period. How a farm bill, if it is passed, will affect the price of ethanol in the future is not really something that a day trader cares that much about.

However, having some knowledge about the fundamentals of a particular stock, or the basic factors that are going to affect how the supply and the demand of a security are going to do in all markets, can really help a day trader respond to various news events that they hear in the day. In addition, some day traders choose to switch their strategy a bit on occasion and go over to the swing trading strategy because they find that it will provide them more profits during that particular trade.

But knowing too much information about a company can be a challenge when it comes to a day trader. They don't need to know who runs the company, about big management changes, how the finances are doing, or any of that. In fact, many day traders can enter and exit the market without finding out about any of this information at all. Outside of little news releases and how that information will affect the stock and the market over the next few hours, they don't need the fundamental analysis that much, which is why you won't see it much in the day trading strategies.

Knowing a little bit about the fundamentals about a company can help in some cases but often it can slow down your day trading process. If you plan to trade daily in one or two particular stocks because they seem to follow the strategy you are going with, take some time to learn a few of these fundamentals. This will help you to notice when trends are changing and can keep you on the lookout for any big news events that can get you ahead of the game. Otherwise, it is probably not really worth your time to look at the fundamental analysis as a day trader.

Technical Analysis (TA)

The technical analysis is going to work slightly different than what you find with the fundamental analysis. The fundamental analysis is going to look at the financial statements and more of a company to determine what the fair value of the business is, compared to what it is selling for on the stock market. With a technical analysis, the trader is going to assume that the price of the company's stock is already reflecting its value and then will keep its focus on statistical analysis of price movements.

A technical analysis is sometimes seen as complicated, but it basically has you look at graphs and determine the best time to enter into the market with your day trading. You can look at a lot of the different strategies that we showed in this guidebook and see a lot of options on how to do a technical analysis.

The technical analysis is going to be a method of evaluating stocks. It is going to use a statistical analysis of the activity in the market such as volume and price. The trader who uses this is not going to attempt to measure the intrinsic value of a security. Instead, they will use a variety of tools and other charts in order to find patterns they can use for their own investment decisions. There are actually quite a few different types of technical analysis. Some are going to rely on patterns that are found in a chart, others are going to use technical oscillators and indicators. Most traders are going to use some combination of these techniques. In any case, you would use historical price and volume data to help make decisions which are not seen with a fundamental analysis.

There are three assumptions that come with a technical analysis. These assumptions include:

• History is often going to repeat itself.

• The price tends to move in a trend.

• The market is going to discount everything.

Before we move on here, realize there are a lot of different options when you do a technical analysis. You can get things like chart patterns or a statistical indicator. With all of the strategies that we talked about earlier, you can look and see that a technical analysis takes many different forms.

The Value of TA in Day Trading

The Market Is Going to Discount out Everything

Many experts are going to criticize this kind of analysis because it is only going to consider the movements in price while completely ignoring all of the fundamental factors that should be behind these decisions. But if you are a day trader who just wants to take advantage of some of the price movements that happen in the market, then this is not a bad thing.

As a technical analyst, you go into the market believing that everything from the fundamentals of a company to broad market factors and even the market psychology of the company is already going to be shown in the price of the stock. This is an important factor because it explains why a technical analyst is not going to concern themselves with the fundamental factors before they make decisions for investing. They assume that it is all tied together and then reflected in the price that the charts show.

Since all of this information is shown inside the current market price of the security, the only thing that is left for a trader is to analyze the price movements. These movements are not so much related to the company at that time but more related to the supply and the demand for that stock in the market at that time. If the day trader can estimate the supply and demand right at certain points during the day, they can translate that into some good profits.

Prices Tend to Move in a Trend

As a technical analysis, you are going to learn that the price for a stock is going to move in some kind of trend. This is sometimes a short-term, mid-term, or long-term trend. This means that the price of a stock is more likely to continue a past trend rather than move around erratically. It will only get off this trend if some big even happens that pushes it there which is why many day traders keep an eye on the news during their trades. Most technical trading strategies are based on the assumption that the price will move in a trend.

History Is Often Going to Repeat Itself

Those who decide to work with the technical analysis are going to believe that history will repeat itself even when it comes to the stock market. The repetitive nature of these movements in price will be attributed to market psychology. These trends are very predictable and can be followed, and they will be based on the emotions of other traders, including emotions like excitement or fear.

A technical analysis is going to use some chart patterns to help them predict and analyze these emotions, as well as the movements in the market that come from these emotions, in order to understand the trends seen on the chart. While there are many forms of this technical analysis that have been used for more than 100 years, they are relevant because they show how these patterns in price movements will repeat themselves over and over again.

If you believe that the movement of price is going to keep up with the same trends that it did throughout history, then you can use this information to help you make informed decisions to help you reach the right investment options. This may take a little bit of time to accomplish, but with some research and some notes, you can use that same information to help you make smart decisions for your investments for a long time to come.

The Aim of TA

As an investor, you can easily work with either of these types of analysis. But while long-term investments can come up with some options that work great under either of these options, most day traders will just stick with the technical analysis, mainly because they don't care about the long-term implications of the stock and the information from this analysis is enough for their type of trading.

Most of the strategies that come with day trading will rely on these technical analyses, and you basically just look at the charts surrounding the stock and make informed decisions based on that information. There are different ways to do this, you simply need to explore some of the other day trading strategies and pick the one that works best for you.

When Technical Analysis Fails

Many traders depend so hugely on technical indicators that they fail to recognize that signs come from price, so when you employ technical indicators, you include a new stratum of analysis between you and the price. Here is some common mistake that traders make when using technical analysis and how to avoid them:

• Not making use of your eyes more: the best indicators of price movements are your eyes, there is no distortion or obstacle between indicators and the price. Hence, before you make use of advanced strategies and signs, you should consider that each indicator included in your chart builds an obstacle between your natural visual senses and price. This form of reasoning can save you from errors in your decision making, especially if you're a beginner trade. So, it's best to leave it basic and begin with simple and straightforward visual analysis.

• Forgetting some time frame analysis: one of the greatest mistakes made by some traders when using technical analysis, and chart analysis and patterns are forgetting weekly time frame analysis as they consider the daily time frame analysis. The number of clues and hints you can obtain by studying both the daily charts and the weekly charts is shocking. The relevance of your review is subject to the amount of time frame that you employ in your analysis. Your chart analysis will be less meaningful when you have a shorter time frame. Studying weekly charts will allow you see fundamentals better, and you also get to view the actual resistance and support lines that have an authentic meaning attached to them, because they were able to last a long period within being removed. Most experienced traders start their analysis with weekly charts and study primary trend and strength. Then they carefully journey to the daily charts and ensure that the trend is going in the same direction. Then they go on to studying day trade charts and start setting out potential exits and entry points. Following this procedure will drastically cause your analysis to change as you advance towards the daily time frame. Therefore, before making use of ambiguous and complicated technical indicators, learn visual technical analysis and make use of your eyes more. When you have adequately mastered the act of identifying charts, then you can make use of technical indicators. It's always better to begin trading with new charts. Understand that some of the top traders in the globe depend more on their eyes and do not even make use of most technical indicators. Ensure your analysis considers different time frames; don't be under the assumption that simply because you are a day trader, you don't need daily and weekly charts or that they are less relevant or useful to your trades. This tip is mainly associated with indexes and broad market since stocks tend to adhere to indexes about 70% of the time. As a day trader, you must see yourself as a technical trader. You must learn to rely more on price action and charts to guide your decision making. Do not overemphasize solely on volume. Have a good understanding of how to factor in volume to your trades.

Conclusion

Congratulations! You have now completed one of the most comprehensive books about day trading for beginners. You should now feel ready to begin your new career as a day trader.

By now, you have gained more insight on day trading than you had when you picked up this book. Not only do you know what day trading is, but you know what a typical day is like for a trader. On top of this, you know a few bonus tips on how to manage your time, you know several common mistakes that day traders make (that you can now avoid), and you know the right mindset that you have to work towards in order to reach success as a trader.

Of course, you have also learned different day trading strategies and platforms that are commonly used. You have learned about the steps you need to take before you begin trading, such as creating your business or trading plan and all the research that goes into learning about the profession. You have also read about creating a watchlist, how important your trading plan is, and how to execute your trading plan when you begin your day trading journey.

This book also touched on a few stocks that many day traders look at throughout their day and factors that will help you in choosing the best stocks for you. Furthermore, you have learned that there are different types of brokers, how to find the best broker, and the rights you have when it comes to working with your chosen broker.

Although this is a comprehensive beginner's book, your research and learning journey as a day trader is not over. There are many other resources that you can investigate, including the resources included in this book. I want to see you succeed in your day trading career and, therefore, I hope that you will take the information from this book with you as you begin your journey. Best wishes and happy trading!

CPSIA information can be obtained
at www.ICGtesting.com
Printed in the USA
LVHW051311080121
675636LV00003B/327

9 781801 129701